Lost to the Sea

For Kate Walker

Lost to the Sea

Britain's Vanished Coastal Communities: The Yorkshire Coast & Holderness

Stephen Wade

PEN & SWORD HISTORY

First published in Great Britain in 2017 by
Pen & Sword History
an imprint of
Pen & Sword Books Ltd
47 Church Street
Barnsley
South Yorkshire
S70 2AS

ISBN 978 1 47389 343 6

A CIP catalogue record for this book is available from the British
Library

Typeset in Ehrhardt by
Mac Style Ltd, Bridlington, East Yorkshire

Printed and bound in Malta by Gutenberg Press Ltd.

Pen & Sword Books Ltd incorporates the imprints of Pen & Sword
Archaeology, Atlas, Aviation, Battleground, Discovery, Family History,
History, Maritime, Military, Naval, Politics, Railways, Select, Transport,
True Crime, Fiction, Frontline Books, Leo Cooper, Praetorian Press,
Seaforth Publishing and Wharncliffe.

For a complete list of Pen & Sword titles please contact
PEN & SWORD BOOKS LIMITED
47 Church Street, Barnsley, South Yorkshire, S70 2AS, England
E-mail: enquiries@pen-and-sword.co.uk
Website: www.pen-and-sword.co.uk

Contents

Introduction

Full many a gem of purest ray serene
The dark unfathomed caves of ocean bear.
Thomas Gray, *Elegy in a Country Churchyard*

They missed out on our island's story; they were erased from the records; if they had diarists or chroniclers, then they disappeared too. They were towns or villages or mere clusters of homesteads perhaps given the name 'hamlet' by passing writers or visitors. Once, they had streets where carts rattled on cobbles or on caked mud; they were homes echoing with laughter, teasing and commands. Children played in the roads and fields. These places missed out, though, on the tales of the bigger picture. In fact, in later times, ships sailed over their remains, not by them, and as the years passed, scraps of driftwood cracked into their walls and broken fishing ships lodged in their old stone fragments after the smaller scale materials had drifted down 60 miles of coast to gather as shingle beach at Spurn, or perhaps much went further south to Lincolnshire.

They are the communities lost to the North Sea, or, as it was known until the twentieth century, the German Ocean. When we stare out onto the restless immensity today, we have to concede that *ocean* is the proper name for it, at least when words are on paper. Generally though, it is a sea, and it has been hungry for land since several thousand years BC.

If we have a clue from today's maps as to what the geography once was, before so many places tumbled into watery oblivion, it is in the place names. The towns ending in *–sey* such as Withernsea, Hornsea and Skipsea, were once alongside lakes, or 'meres', as they were called in Yorkshire. Only Hornsea Mere survives of the lakes that were once there in the Mesolithic times, when hunter-gatherers would find freshwater fish there. The *–sey* suffix indicates a lake, and perhaps their size was indicated in the word itself, which relates to the German 'Meer', meaning sea.

To try to understand the appearance of these sunken places is a tough challenge. There are clues sometimes in the spindrift on the shore; old drawings and photographs offer a little help, but overall the attempt to describe and convey what lies under the waves depends on science – mainly on maritime archaeology. But of course, the sunken places are disintegrated: they have dissolved and been dragged away by the tides. A search for a Yorkshire Atlantis would be fruitless.

The subject of these lost places has spun its own stories. Where only partial knowledge exists, folklore and hearsay step into the vacuum. Every submerged town seems to have its ghostly church bells, just as ghost stories of shipwrecks have their spectral cries of the drowned. Our imaginations want to see the disappeared places existing as they were when they were on land, but of course, that is a poetic vision, not a reality.

Most of them now exist as names on old maps, and a search for their nature often leads to no more than a bare list of names of farms, chapels, barns or beacons. They resist a full description, but the impulse to look further and dig around for a little more substance is irresistible.

These places lost to the sea have another appeal to the imagination: the notion of the unfinished. Unfinished symphonies and incomplete novels have their own mesmeric fascination. Charles Dickens's *The Mystery of Edwin Drood* calls out for writers to supply an ending. Many have tried to do so. But in the case of lost towns, we have unfinished stories and there is no possibility of an artificial ending. We will never know the destiny of Ravenser Odd, now sunk on the seabed off Spurn.

It is almost as if these places evaded history, as the waves engulfed them, rubbed them out. Lost medieval villages inland are there in vestigial form. Geophysical gadgets and aerial photography reveal their substance and extent. But the sea not only swallows these fated homes and lives: it shrouds them at once in both obscurity and mystery. The result is a riddle, something as compelling as a criminal case for Sherlock Holmes.

In the end, science appears to be frustrated by the limitations of its enquiry. In most cases, the fruits of seabed research seem destined to be limited to descriptive and factual listings and catalogues. Fortunately, though, archaeology has now joined the new social historical writing in its ability to evoke and revivify the materials in the sedimentary layers of silt and shingle. The divers have joined the analysts and the *Time Team* methodology has spread, so that stories emerge from bones and artefacts, albeit very slowly. Often, the remains beneath the water are not so deeply bedded either. In August 2016, a party led by Dr Goncharov in Russia found the remains of *The Thames*, a ship lost on its way to Siberia in 1878. Goncharov commented, 'We had sonar and cameras but the water is very murky there so we didn't get a good resolution. We did a few dives and there it was.'

Along the Yorkshire coast, below Flamborough all the way down to Spurn, the lost towns or villages are not there, even as mere stone and mud in some cases, below the waves; they are fragments on the long stretch of Spurn Point. In 1912, Thomas Sheppard, a museum curator and amateur geologist, listed them all, shown on one of his maps. They were, going from north to south: Wilsthorpe, Auburn, Hartburn, Hyde, Withow, Cleton, Northorpe, Hornsea Burton, Hornsea Beck, Southorpe, Great Colden, Colden Parva, Old Aldborough, Ring borough, Monkwell, Monkwike, Sand-le-Mere, Waxhole, Owthorne by Sisterkirk, Newsome, Old Withernsea, Out Newton, Dimlington, Turmarr, Northorp, Hoton, Old Kilnsea, Ravensprun and Ravenser Odd.

Sheppard's map shows also the position of the Roman coastline, confirming my earlier reference to the fact that 3½ miles have been lost since the first century AD. The following chapters will tell the stories of most of these lost settlements. I have omitted merely one or two that were never more than a farm or some other single building.

In 1930, printed in a guide book to Filey and surrounding places, we have this statement:

> But for protective works, Hornsea would soon be described, like so many other places on this coastline, as lost to the sea. The town has already contributed a hotel and a former suburb, Hornsea Beck, to the devouring ocean. In 1907, a substantial sea wall, with a double promenade, extending for about 900 feet, was completed, and it is hoped that this will stay the ravages of the sea for many years.

Such comforting assertions have been made through the centuries about that coast, and yet the North Sea, or the German Ocean, as it was once known, is still hungry for more Yorkshire land.

Today, we are far less confident, and the worrying carries on year after year. In 2012, Martin Wainwright, in *The Guardian*, expressed the kind of thinking everyone surely experiences when they look out from the Yorkshire coast from a crumbling cliff:

> More properties which now all but teeter above the beach below have been added to the list of homes no longer considered safe. Retired couples in Aldborough, 1k south of Hornsea, face almost certain evacuation before next summer. Ten houses were abandoned last year.

The daily papers also disturb us with the bigger picture, describing such things as global warming and the melting of the Arctic ice cap. In 2015, for instance, *The Independent* stated, 'Greenland's ice sheet began melting so early this year that scientists monitoring it thought they had made a mistake. … The melting covers an area of 656,000 square miles and is the result of unusually warm weather.' In January 2016, *National Geographic* magazine asked of the general reader: 'The Arctic ice pack is dwindling. What will it do to the planet?' Fortunately, the experts featured in the article explain that there is no certainty about the effects of this on coastlines: 'How a rapidly warming Arctic will influence weather across the hemisphere is a bit hazier.' But in the popular, lay imagination, people tend to envisage the ice cap melting and the coast nearest to them being engulfed in proportion to the big melt up north. Fortunately, it is not as simple as that.

In fact, the question of coastal erosion and the loss of homes to the sea invites dark, restless arithmetic. It is one of those subjects that actually commandeer maths in order to strike the note of high drama. Photographers rush to get that last snap of the house hanging over the cliff edge.

This book is a social history of the lives of people in communities all along this coast, from Scarborough down to the Humber estuary, and it started with the shock of seeing a man with only a few square feet of lawn left mowing his patch, with the sea raging just feet away. After seeing this, at Skipsea, I knew I had to write this book.

When the poet Philip Larkin reached the status of literary celebrity in the early 1960s, he was librarian at the University of Hull. Larkin had a strong aversion to publicity and told his friends that if a journalist arrived, looking for him, his assistant could tell the stranger that Larkin wasn't there, and it would be better to carry on north and interview Basil Bunting in Newcastle. Larkin knew that being in Hull was a life 'near the end of land', as he put it. To southerners, he thought, anywhere considered to be 'north' was very much the same and was on the wild side, bordering the infinite sea.

Larkin knew that Hull nudged the flat and melancholy land known as Holderness. If the traveller carries on past Hull going east, he will pass through Hedon and then go out into little villages whose names make it clear that the Vikings were here once. 'The end of land' is indeed almost a domain of the sea, and has always struggled to keep any human roots it may have, and the chronicles of that stretch of Yorkshire from Flamborough Head to the north to Spurn to the south show a constant battle with the elements, most dramatically, with the hungry sea.

In my childhood, my relatives from the West Riding had their annual summer holidays by the sea, along with thousands of other slaves of the 'dark, satanic mills' and many other industries. The family photo album shows the adults sitting on benches, swathed in dark clothes, staring out at the sea. We children, playing endless games of cricket on the beach at Blackpool, Morecambe, Filey or Bridlington, were aware of the sea as a border to the playground of sand, but at moments of strong emotion and shivering imagination, the Irish Sea or the North Sea was also a massive, brooding pool of danger as well as of solace. Yes, the sea was for swimming and clowning with cousins, but it was also the home of the jellyfish on one mundane level of danger, and the abode of something more mythic, more belonging to the world of fable and old family tales.

The British love of staring at the sea became the accompaniment to those summer escapes. Growing up, I looked more closely at those adult stares, the gaping out into the grey infinitude; later, I absorbed the same trancelike thrall. Trying to rationalize this enchantment, I slowly began to see that, though the feelings were never expressed, the stare was into something timeless, elemental – the kind of look the human gives to nature's double-sided treasure, a threat softened by a dream. Yes, there were fishing boats, and yes, there were always tales of the sea, as in my father's stories of being a stoker in minesweepers in the Second World War. One summer's day, a submarine anchored in Filey Bay, and I was rowed out, with a dozen other kids, to board her and step down into her bosom, guided by my dad. I remember that frisson of fear with the sense that I was standing beneath the waves, and that the great seething watery beast was stretched out above me.

This was all about the draw of a subterranean world, of course – a reminder of the truth of the line, *tempus edax rerum*, time actually 'eating or consuming' all things, but it also entails a revision of the idea of nature. It is as if we feel a need to personify, as in 'Mother Nature', but now, that stare and fascination is with the dark side of that elemental force. Still, we know that this attempt to create some kind of mythic natural power is a clear example of the pathetic fallacy: that is, we don't wish to accept fully and coldly the fact that mutability is more powerful than our feeble little notions of what 'life' and 'time' are.

I have found that the new writing that seeks to relate imagery of nature to both the process of history and the mysteries of topography opens up some wider thinking about the human experience through time. We distil our fears and limitations down to proverbs and adages, happy to let a cliché stand in place of a profound feeling of dread. The fact is that the people beneath the waves, their past lives, ambitions and dreams, are not fully lost. They are suspended in liquid, merely a larger version of the specimens pickled in the biology lab jars. In more approachable terms, these lost communities have an unfinished story, of course. There beneath the water are the remains of a place, its people on the way to being something else.

But my curiosity about the realm of the sea came later. In my student reading, the sea became a presence in English literature, seeping into the English sensibility almost as much as the Biblical narrative and its persistent metaphors. Reading, walking and learning, with Cardigan Bay now as the maritime backdrop, I registered the old sentence about no place in England being more than 70 miles from the sea; it seemed pointless to be comforted by that, when I watched massive waves rumble into the sea front at Aberystwyth and lash the roof and balconies of the lofty Victorian Alexandra Hall, which crouched beneath the cliff on the north side of the bay.

Student reading brought a deepening of my interest in English communities and social change, and how history had shown that even the strongest and deepest roots of places were easily wrenched out, smashed or engulfed. Greediest of all forces for social and material change was water. In Wales, Lake Vyrnwy had been made into a reservoir to give water to Liverpool; the village of Llanwddyn was flooded and wiped out of history. Nearer home, in Yorkshire, older people spoke of floods on the Norfolk coast and of villages being utterly destroyed.

My interest was placed down behind other concerns, but only until I came to live in Lincolnshire: now I was in a place that knew all about the tendency of the North Sea to erase people, homes and entire communities. That immensity of water, as those in thrall by the sea know very well, covers not only layers of rock from past eras; it also has vestiges of the human element. Out there, in the North Sea, is what is now called Doggerland. Around 6,000 BCE, a sea shelf slipped, to the north of Britain, and water rushed into what was a bridge between Britain and Europe. In this way, some of the very first settlements claimed by the sea were made. Around the coastline generally, traces of the former settlements and land features are sometimes seen. Perhaps one of the most extraordinary instances of this was when Nick Crane, making the television series *Coast*, had this experience on the Severn Estuary:

> As the mud was being eroded by the waters of the Severn, it was breaking into layers, each layer representing a deposit of silt laid down by a particular tide, more than 8,000 years ago. One of the layers was covered with footprints; tiny, human footprints. They were so clear that they might have been made ten minutes earlier.

Usually, what we see when these rare glimpses occur is vegetation, as in the ancient forest that appears off the coast at Borth, in Mid-Wales. But those footprints somehow signified the mystery of the enveloping sea.

The curiosity began when I found a great slab of rock containing a trilobite beneath the cliffs of the north beach at Filey, in North Yorkshire. I have always been an explorer of seashores, spending hours turning over stones, yearning to see imprinted or imprisoned insects or plants pressed into them.

It is a fascination from boyhood holidays in Filey, when the Brigg – a long ridge of solid igneous rock extending into the North Sea from the town – was the majestic northern boundary for beachcombers such as me. The Brigg still stands, but the half-mile of clay between the base of the Brigg and the landing platform where the fishing boats known as cobles used to stand in lines back in the 1960s, is now so eroded that an area the size of a football pitch has been taken back by the waves.

There above me were the soggy cliff lines of geologists' treasures and little boys' wonder: the shells, the multifarious scraps from the waves' rages, from abalone fragments glistening pink to the shiny weathered pebbles of the sedimentary layers, some as if brushed and sprayed clear, and others somehow clouded, deadened, by time and weather. I felt a shiver of dread ripple through me, looking upwards at the denuded browny surface. It was as if some giant's mouth had been sliced off to reveal a claggy throat embedded with scraps of food after a feast.

My questions then began, after seeing the alarming extent of the meal being enjoyed by the voracious sea. The whole of the Holderness coast, down from Filey to the long tongue of Spurn Head, was open to the sea's rages. With alarming frequency, reports on the evening local news for Yorkshire told of yet another home gradually melting into the sea. The most dramatic images were those in which wholesome and rather pastoral cottages bordering pasture were shown: there was the family home, with a tiny rose-adorned garden and part of a field beyond. What had once been a tilled field of many acres was now, in these pictures, a little fringe of grass with a sharp drop down to the sea's edge. The family looked out onto this shrunken greenness and saw the expanse of the North Sea beyond. This is going on all the time. The sea encroaches and nothing can be done.

This long arching coastal stretch down to Spurn, which stretches out so that its point is seen from Cleethorpes on the opposite North Lincolnshire coast, has a line of coastal villages, all living – to use an apposite cliché – on the edge. In 1930, one guidebook writer noted that the little village of Hornsea, 15 miles south of Bridlington, was vulnerable, and his optimism is plaintively sad:

But for protective works, Hornsea would soon be described, like so many other places on this coastline, as 'Lost by the Sea'. The town has already contributed a hotel and a former suburb, Hornsea Beck, to the devouring ocean. In 1907, a substantial sea wall, with a double promenade, extending for about 900 feet, was completed, and it is hoped that this will stay the ravages of the sea for many years.

The consensus appears to be that there is an acceptable arithmetic of loss regarding Holderness and its fate. The loss of land is around 9 feet a year, and if we change that to an estimate as to how much land has tumbled into the waves, we might say that 2 million tons of earth are lost each year. As one writer said, in 1930, 'If the loss has been continuous, no less than 66,600 acres of our tight little island must have disappeared in this locality alone since the Roman invasion under Julius Caesar.'

At the other end, the bend of land that makes Spurn and Spurn Head stretches around 3 miles from Kilnsea to the tip of land, and in the wide bay created in the gap of land that was once a cluster of villages, we have the Easington clays and the Kilnsea clays. The place names of the landmarks signifying the geography of disappearance resound with the fear of non-being beneath the layers of history: there are Old Den and Greedy Gut, for instance, to the south of the Kilnsea clays.

Back in 1849, the Spurn peninsula, which was the only creation of new land over the centuries since the last villages were inundated in the late Middle Ages, a terrific gale blasted the gathered shingle and made a string of small islands that appeared at high tide. Twenty years later, groynes were in place and a solid bank of chalk was created, being the base of the future Spurn Point. Spurn may have been the only new land accrued as the villages in its arch and to its north were destroyed, but even Spurn has been under constant threat. Thirty years ago, Kenneth Hartley noted, 'No comparable cases of breaches have occurred since these works were completed, although the threat increases with each passing year.'

By the 1920s, photographs of Spurn show the latest lighthouse, crew houses for the lifeboat and vestiges of a fort. Most significantly perhaps is the arrival of a railway. The Spurn Head Railway was established just before the Great War, and then the developments were made to back up the line. At

Kilnsea there were barracks and a hospital, to house the military personnel billeted in the area to guard the North Sea. A few miles north at the village of Roos, there was J.R.R. Tolkien, who was posted there after coming back injured from the Front. The place was always vulnerable: between the high tide mark and the cliff house to the west of Kilnsea, the distance of the Easington Road was just over 1,000 yards – the widest point of the peninsula.

Inside that bend of land, west of Kilnsea as well as south, the lost villages of Holderness lay beneath the waves. Under those wide flats, as the Spurn Railway was being built, were the settlements of Orwithfleet, Scunthorpe, Ravensar and Ravensar Odd. Of these places, Ravensar Odd has attracted most historical interest. This trading town was a major seaport before the growth of Hull. The Humber floods did not hit the place until the mid-fourteenth century; before then, it was an important port and had its own MP. An inquisition of Edward III contains this information in a writ to the servants responsible for tax-gathering in his domain:

> Whereas recently we have learned that the town has been daily diminished by frequent inundations of the water of the sea surrounding the said town, and the soil there of great quantity has been carried away, and that 145 buildings which belong to Cecily de Selby ... and forty-two places not built upon ... which said buildings and places constituted two parts and more of the aforesaid town, have been taken by the sea by such inundations and the flux of the said waters, from the eighth year of King Edward ... and the people have withdrawn from that town by reason of such waste and impoverishment that they are not able in any way to support or pay the tenths and tolls.

The King was tolerant. He asked for only 100 shillings. But as is easily inferred from this, Ravenser Odd was a large-scale community. In fact, despite the fact that in the Domesday Book of 1086 there were no Holderness boroughs, by about 1250, there were three – Hedon and Skipsea, along with Ravenser Odd. These places were founded by the family of Aumale, who had been given burgage charters by the English kings. This meant that the landowners of the locality held land by paying an annual rent to the sovereign; this was not fully abolished until 1925.

Ravenser Odd is one of many ports recorded in this area in early times. One of the most vague and elusive is 'Cornu Vallis', which was a Saxon port referred to by Ceolfrid's scribe back in the seventh century. All we know of it today, as landscape archaeologist Richard Muir has put it, is that 'it is lost'. Ravenser itself figures prominently in the story of 1066, however; it was from here (then called Hrafnseri in Old English) that Harald Hardrada sailed home after being defeated just outside York at Stamford Bridge in that year, before Harold sped down south to his doom at Hastings.

Ravenser Odd has gone, but along the Holderness coast, the line of villages on the edge of the land continues to provide stories of threatened dissolution and ruin. One of the most striking declines has been the story of Skipsea. Here was a notable castle, built by Drogo de la Beuvriere, and although its demolition was ordered in 1221, the place was always important because of the notion of castle guard. This phrase defined the military holding, created after the 1066 conquest, in the framework of Norman power across the land. This meant that the holder of the castle guard tenure acted for the King. In the 1200s, knights in Holderness gave knight service and castle guard to their sovereign. In the early medieval centuries, records give mention to the castle guard at Skipsea.

Skipsea was once the main residence of the Lord of Holderness; forty years ago, a local writer noted that the place was then 'little more than an uneasy summer retreat of chalets and bungalows perched precariously above the beach'. Today, as a newspaper report stated in 2011, the situation there is that at least twenty homes will be in the sea within the next century. Between Flamborough and Spurn – 45 miles – it has been estimated that 200 homes are under threat. The University of Hull has gathered a collection of photos giving evidence of the sea's devouring of coastal roads, and academics there have been busy estimating the rate of land loss over the next decades.

Nearby Hornsea is full of historical interest, and owes its popularity as a resort chiefly to a Hull entrepreneur called Joseph Wade. His cash from a timber company helped to finance the building of a railway from Hull to Hornsea, opened in 1864. But Hornsea, now perhaps most famous for its pottery, goes back a very long way as a settlement. In the late fourteenth century it was the fifth largest place in the East Riding of Yorkshire.

Erosion is a constant threat, and a related settlement, Hornsea Beck, has been completely lost and is on the list of the ghostly former villages of Holderness; it was first mentioned in 1228, and not long after that there was a weekly market, part of a charter gained by St Mary's Abbey. Poll Tax records show a population of 264 people in 1377 – a slightly larger number than that of Hornsea itself. It was in the fifteenth century that erosion began to be a problem. It has been calculated that from 1546 to 1609, thirty-eight properties were lost to the waves. One of the ways in which we know of a footnote in the historical record is through legal documents, and sure enough, it is the court rolls that in this case indicate that Hornsea Beck was close to its final stage of decline in the mid-eighteenth century.

In 2011, the north country journalist and writer Martin Wainwright wrote a feature for *The Guardian* (quoted in my introduction) on the Holderness lost villages, and he listed twenty-nine lost villages; these had first been listed by Thomas Sheppard, writing in 1912. The erosion problems are at a desperate stage, yet as Wainwright notes, there is just one consolation – at least for Lincolnshire people – that 'much of the debris from the coast is washed round Spurn Point and into the Humber, reinforcing the delicate-looking peninsula and creating new land from the estuary in the area of Sunk Island.'

If we have to pinpoint one place that contains all the woes and trials of being potentially a village lost in the sea, we go to Aldborough, just 6 miles south of Hornsea. Already, three hotels have fallen into the sea – The Spa, The Talbot and The Royal. Old Aldborough has already gone. Today, the seaside road has been eaten away and is blocked off at the cliff edge. The British Geological Survey is giving the place a great deal of attention.

The Survey records that 'The cliffs are receding and the cliff profile is stepped due to the contrasting erosion resistances of the tills ... in some cases, middle sections of the cliff are subject to considerable erosion by wave action.' The caravan site has received some attention also; the Survey authors conclude that a study of maps shows that 'using data going back to 1786, up to 2 million square metres a year were removed from the cliff.' There have also been, naturally, severe landslides.

Looking at the historical records for Aldbrough, the efforts in the Victorian years to develop the place as a seaside holiday location were adventurous and optimistic, but met with little success. In 1832, there was a beer house near the sea. Robert Raikes began to build a hotel at that time, and that became The Talbot; sea bathing began, and from 1846, The Spa Inn was established. There were attempts to lift the place into the category of spa town. There was an omnibus service from Hull in the 1840s, and three lodging houses are recorded then. But its competitor, Hornsea, won the race for the title of a 'seaside place for Hull'.

Holderness and its lost villages provide an intensive case study for understanding the patterns of loss regarding the villages now under the sea. In part a story of medieval rise and fall, and in part a more modern tale of technology versus the rapid erosion, the Holderness chronicle of communities against the North Sea is one in which small numbers battle with all resources against the inevitable mutability of sea and land in geomorphological change. If we need to see this struggle encapsulated in one microcosmic instance, it is in the determined striving of the monks of Meaux Abbey. This was Cistercian, founded in 1151 by William le Gros. It was one of the many victims of Henry VIII's ravages, closing in 1539.

We know from a chronicle written by Thomas de Burton that the middle years of the fourteenth century were hard in the extreme for the brothers. The record says:

> The waters of the Humber, by its flood-like inundations, had wasted our land at Tharlsthorpe and we were known to be unable … on account of other misfortunes … to bear the maintenance and repair of those banks which defended our land.

The monks were repeatedly building new defensive banks, but the sea kept on destroying their work. In about 1400, after lots more work on defensive banks, the Abbey grange at Tharlsthorp was no more. The place was on the growing list of former locations – a place name without a place.

The melancholy vista is there for anyone walking the shore, particularly between Spurn and the land just east of Hedon. The long arch of mud refuses to have any changing identity but colour. Landscape is irrelevant: what the humans who stare to sea see here is a reluctant acceptance that there can only be one winner in this struggle. In 1861, the historian John Mayhall provided one of the most powerful summaries of what devastation could be worked by the sea. Referring to 1607, to a nationwide disaster, he wrote:

A terrible flood devastated the south-western counties of England and Wales, whereby twenty-six parishes in Monmouthshire were entirely swept away, and the counties of Somerset, Gloucester, Glamorgan, Cardigan and Carmarthen were fearfully overflown by the sea. 500 persons perished and thousands were utterly ruined. The counties of Lincoln, Norfolk, Huntingdon and Kent were similarly visited in the most sudden manner.

Holderness was not alone in its sufferings.

Today, though, the loss of land to the sea is more visible and more speedily known. Whereas in the past the loss was stealthy until the day a massive inundation came, now the best brains in applied science are at work to tackle the problem. But it seems certain that more villages will eventually be lost to the sea, and some will be on the Holderness coast.

The walker today can either view the vastness of the estuary from the north bank, or stand just south of Cleethorpes on the Lincolnshire coast and see the tip of Spurn, but the view will be dominated by the Humber forts, one of which is almost near enough to touch, one feels, staring out from the Fitties sand dunes at Humberston. The forts remind us that the Great War brought another threat to this coast – the Zeppelin bombs and the mines laid by the German navy. On the east coast, Scarborough and Hartlepool were bombed and there was loss of life, and at Cleethorpes, a church was hit at a time when there was a gathering of soldiers stationed there. Many died.

This is a reminder that the coast from Bridlington to Cleethorpes has had to deal with the lashing of the sea, but there have been other threats as well. Somehow, as I thought on my last visit to the North Lincolnshire coast, there is a firm resolve here that man will not give up more earth without a fight.

Note: As there is a need to use a certain specialized vocabulary in the text, there are brief explanations where suitable, but fuller definitions are in the glossary.

Chapter 1

Early Historical and Human Experience

That great dust-heap called 'history'.
Augustine Birrell in Thomas Carlyle's
Obiter Dicta

These chapters reflect a quest to somehow reassemble, at least in the mind, a massive amount of atomized materials: there were once homes and families; there were once community ties and aspirations, and these existed inside stone walls or red brick. Before that there were people moving around, somewhere in that distant and textless history we call 'prehistory'. In fact, there is one long continuity of human experience, only because there is a need for writers and historians to define, compartmentalize and label segments of time that the general reader had tended to separate the humanity found in houses, forts and factories from those who had homes dug into cliffs or mountainsides.

There is history as established consensus: most agree on an interpretation and then the textbooks and websites follow, but there is also the history of things, of material life. I knew from the start that the people whose home soil was stolen by the sea's rages would shift elsewhere, or in the case of the time millennia before the beginning of what we call the Christian era, would perhaps run for their lives as nature faced them with extinction. That is why my materials for this history of loss are fragments, but something tangible may be assembled from scraps and trifles. I had to believe that from the start of these enquiries in what has gone and what remains.

I would like to begin with a short account of something entirely opposed to anything analytical or intellectual. It is an artefact. After all, the people behind the following loosely connected facts and incidents were people who worked with their hands. I like to think that something worthwhile might come from exploring on the page, as well as on the land. I have of course walked all the cliffs and shores mentioned in this history, apart from some of the places marked as 'dangerous', and surely that awful word leads to reflections on what has been faced through the centuries by all those people who faced the North Sea, knowing that their provider would one day become their destroyer.

My own involvement with the North Sea began with a flint: most likely half an axe head. It sits on my desk today, after many years of life moved around from shelf to shelf among my books and pictures. Before that, it was found on the beach at Filey. It is about 1 inch by 1½, and it's reminiscent of a cartoon dog's bone, cut neatly at one side, but on the other it is worked and chipped into that distinctive triangle that suggests a multi tool. I like to think it was carried and used by a man sometime around 10,000 years ago, maybe to slice an animal pelt. Whatever its origin, I'm sure that its maker was lost to the sea, along with this tool. But now here it is, born again, with a story for anyone who looks at it and touches it. I would never, ever have the skills required to fashion such a thing, and I often think of that ancient craftsman. Maybe he drew some images with it, telling tales, like myself.

My story of the coast and the sea begins with two documents. The first is a letter home from Private Rene Baxter in 1941, written at Barmston, just south of Bridlington:

Dear Mother,

How are you? I should have written to you before now but I have been the only cook on duty for the last week and as you will see by my address, we have moved. We came here last Thursday and we are stationed at Bridlington Bar, right on top of the cliffs. We are in bungalows and I can see the sea as we are in bed. It really is beautiful here, but dreadfully isolated. We are about 7 miles from Bridlington and the buses don't run too frequently, but we now have a transport provided two or three times a week and I went yesterday. ... We are allowed to go bathing on our own but the officers have formed parties and there is usually one mid-day and 5.30 pm. Of course, a lot depends on the tide, but it never goes far out from here.

The second document is from an account of Charlotte Bronte in Filey, by F.R. Pearson:

The church which Charlotte Bronte visited that Sunday afternoon is more difficult to identify, though its diminutive dimensions seem to indicate the little Norman church at Speeton, which stands windswept and solitary on the high cliffs between Filey and Flamborough Head. ... Four days later we find her writing to Miss Nussey ... 'The sea has all its own grandeur – I walk on the sands a good deal, and try not to feel desolate and melancholy.'

Both passages comment on the sea and the coast being full of wonder, instilling a sense of awe. For the servicewoman, the closeness to the cliff and the tides is part of her working environment; for Charlotte, who at that point had just seen her sister Anne die in Scarborough, the sand and sea are almost mystical, and certainly 'Romantic' in the literary and artistic sense.

These two contrasting testimonies to the North Sea's great bullying tides, with the land at their mercy, hint at the wide spectrum of human experience that has been evident since people first wrote about the place. On the one hand, it is part of a workplace, up close to nature, and to be used. On the other hand, it is distant, powerful, and mythic. Rene Baxter bathes in it and sees the cliff edge from her bed. She sees the beauty, but she is there in wartime, and other factors kick in. Charlotte is there for spiritual solace.

The two angles of perception here have been evident since the first human settlements left any record, from archaeological to literary. This account of the communities of this coast lost to the sea will mix the grand, overarching narrative of how the sea shaped the seashores we have now, and the story of the people who have lived along the coast, from fisher folk to entrepreneurs, and from excursionists to smugglers.

Marine and land archaeology over the last twenty years have shown just how much there is to know about the past cultures who lived on the now disappeared coasts, or in the areas now very close to the current shoreline. More recently, there has been a general interest in the North Sea and its historical phases of settlement, from the Stone Age to the Early Modern period in particular, because so much of that history created the platform on which the modern developments since the Renaissance have stood, from the powerful Hanseatic League on the Baltic and upper North Sea coasts, to the Dutch-British wars of the seventeenth century and then the following

Industrial Revolution. This latter phase of change gave us the Yorkshire coast as we know it from old postcards and travellers' accounts, ranging from the Age of Reason, in which Scarborough grew as a spa town, to the 1950s, when the first large-scale holiday camps arrived, such as the one at Filey, run by Butlin's.

The stretch of land in question, as far as my history is concerned, goes from Port Mulgrave in the north, down to Holderness and Spurn Point, which reaches out into the Humber mouth, and then to the area now known as Sunk Island, a long range of mudflats, beneath which stand a number of lost communities.

The story of that line of coast, which is now being eaten away relentlessly by the sea, begins with an outline of geological change and very early settlement. In fact, it begins as a chronicle of human existence with the Dogger Bank and the glacial epoch, which receded around 8,000 BC. The ice age, known as the Palaeolithic, which had preceded that massive advance of ice (that left a terminal moraine at its southern tip, which provides a great divide across Yorkshire), gave way to the Mesolithic, and in that period, as archaeology has discovered, hunters and fishermen came across a huge land shelf now known as Doggerland. There is an effort of imagination required to think of this ice age, which was over a very long period a series of advances and retreats of a great glacier.

The geologist Richard Fortey gives a vivid description of this in his survey of the British landscape:

> In glacial phases, glaciers deepened valleys which would become lochs, scratched boulders, and scoured mountains which would now be scalloped with corries or cwms [a *corrie* is scooped-out hollow, usually filled with water; a *cwm* is a hanging valley], prolific sands and gravels washed out from the melting glacier front at every spring. Peat accumulated in bogs and preserved the pollen of a rich flora.

When we look at the timescale in the geology textbooks and try to absorb the reality of the lives and places referred to within the all-embracing term of the Neolithic, for instance, we need the experts to bring us down to earth with facts we can relate to. One of the most astounding facts with reference to this period, called by David Miles in a book on the Neolithic, is that farming, of some kind, began around 4,000 BC. That is an astonishing little footnote to that long and gradual emergence of people who settled rather than engaged in hunting and gathering. David Miles calls his book *The Tale of the Axe*; he sees the axes made of jadeite as the real marker that shows that the people settling on this side of the Doggerland bridge had come from the far side of Europe.

Work done by the Humber Wetland Project, with details published in 1993, has established sea level and climatic change features in this post-glacial period, when sea levels varied. The report listed some examples including stretches of coast that relate to sea level rise from 550–350 BC. The term for a period in which sea levels rise is a *transgression*, and the term for when the levels fall is a *regression*, and work continues on these to look for patterns.

If we trace the timeline down through the years from those early Stone Age people, we find that just a few thousand years before the Roman invasion of Claudius in AD 43, the climate was such that forest and marsh were created, places where water dominated and dictated what could be done. In contrast, the land formed of chalk and limestone meant that people could hunt. The culture that emerged in the Mesolithic era has become known as that of the Long Barrow peoples. Lord Harlech, in his book on the archaeology of Northern England, explained:

> In the East Yorkshire uplands the remains of no fewer than twenty-five long barrows are known, as against only one in the Vale of York. Whenever measurable, the skulls found in these long barrows are long and narrow. The long barrows were communal burial places. … With them are found leaf or lozenge-shaped arrowheads, flint axes with rounded butts, flint knives and numerous sherds [*sic*] of smooth, black, round-bottomed pottery.

After this phase came other people, now labelled the 'Beaker' folk, after the distinctive beaker pottery found with their remains. This time reference is now the late to middle Bronze Age – about 1500–1300 BC. Their implements have been found along the Yorkshire coast, except in Holderness, where a different culture was evident. The findings have been such items as swords and spearheads. There is a consensus that through these centuries there was trade in progress with northern Germany and the Lowlands.

By the time we reach the period around 500 BC, there is evidence of a people known as the Hallstatt folk, a Celtic race almost certainly from what is now Austria and Switzerland. This was a community based on working iron; in the 1920s, for instance, at the Castle area in Scarborough, axes and pottery were found that relate to other finds across Europe, and the overall term for these people is La Tene. It is now thought that these were the ancestors of the Brigantes, who fought the Romans in the first century AD, and that this was the race that inhabited Yorkshire, from the East Riding across to the Pennines.

Today, looking out from, say, Filey Brigg, which has Roman connections, into the North Sea, it takes an effort of the imagination to envisage a great land crossing from Europe – one on which people settled, fi shed and hunted. The area had been geologically studied in more detail than ever the Edwardians knew, when the first works on erosion were published, and we know that north of Scarborough, off Robin Hood's Bay and Ravenscar, which is the limit of a massive base of rock called the Cleveland Basin, there is a sub-marine area called the Peak Trough. To the south, after the ice age, there is a fault known as the Howardian-Flamborough Fault Belt, and the land between these two (today's North Yorkshire and Teesside) was lifted when the fault occurred. A fault is a giant crack showing a line of rock either raised or fallen from its sedimentary line.

This concept, stretching across all of Yorkshire apart from Holderness and the West Riding, helps us imagine the event that really starts the long story of the erosion of the Yorkshire coast – a great flood and a fault that raised the land to create the massive cliffs we now see along that coast from Redcar down to Withernsea and Kilnsea.

We are quite accustomed to hearing the word 'Dogger', referring to one of the thirty-one sea areas of the maritime weather forecast for British seamen, but we perhaps have only the vaguest idea where it is. A glance at that chart for the forecast shows it as a block just above another designated 'Humber'. That has now become, more specifically, a name for a vanished mass of land from pre-history.

Doggerland (or as some call it, 'Northsealand') is really the first lost community in my history. It was a massive area of land beginning about 100 miles off Spurn and extending a long way north. Most recent thinking, emanating from the work done at Imperial College London and from research by Gareth Collins and his colleagues, suggest that its end came when there was a 'tsunami' and subsea landslide off Storegga, in Norway, and the argument from these sources is that it was abandoned about 8,000 years ago. The press have insisted on calling Doggerland 'the British Atlantis' but as work has progressed, more and more is beginning to be known about its people. A report by Paul Rincon for BBC News summarizes what it was like:

> By around 20,000 years ago, the area would still have been one of the richest areas for hunting, fishing and fowling in Europe. A large freshwater basin occupied Doggerland, fed by the river Thames from the west and by the Rhine from the east. Its lagoons, marshes and mudflats would have been a haven for wildlife.

Rincon quoted Bernhard Weniger from the University of Cologne: 'In Mesolithic times, this was paradise.' But later, Doggerland was a low-level landscape, and estimates put it as about the size of Wales. The most exciting – and relevant – feature of new research on Doggerland is the evidence of the humans who lived and worked there. Remains and artefacts have been found; traces of the drowned landscapes are gradually becoming better known. The largest evidence is in the 'drowned forests' – groups of tree stumps that occasionally become visible. It seems that this terrain was one of deciduous woods, rivers and mudflats. A feature in *Current Archaeology* journal in 2016 gives an insight into what was there:

> At Tygbrind Vig, off the coast of Denmark, such stunning discoveries as textile fragments, wooden paddles, well-preserved Mesolithic dwellings – some with intact wall stakes – have all been recorded on the sea floor, preserved ironically by the waterlogged conditions that led to these communities being abandoned.

The feature also attempts to describe the intangible: 'Northsealand would have represented not just a home but a storehouse of memories and ideas: the place is evocative, closely tied to memory.' This is exactly what the story of the Yorkshire coast communities has to try to locate, despite its being so fragmentary.

The undersea land had been imagined previously. H.G. Wells, a visionary in his fiction in so many ways, wrote a tale called *A Story of the Stone Age* in 1897. It is about a time when 'one might walk dryshod from France to England, and when a broad and sluggish Thames flowed through its marshes to meet its father Rhine, flowing through a wide and level country that is under water these latter days.' In the early twentieth century, Clement Reid began a search for Neolithic human remains, and he wrote *The Antiquity of Man* in 1913. One of the highlights in the saga of this search for Doggerland was when, in 1931, a ship called the *Colinda*, off Norfolk, brought out of the sea a great peat clod, and within that was a harpoon, dating back to several thousand years BC.

It was Bryony Coles who gave Doggerland its name. She was the first to try to map the hypothetical position of the area. The artefacts are now multiplying; geophysical modelling is being undertaken, and apart from the usual flint tools and such, the occasional find of a more startling nature is located, such as a huge fossilized mammoth bone. One researcher explained:

> We haven't found an 'x marks the spot' or 'Joe created this', but we have found many artefacts and submerged features that are very difficult to explain by natural causes, such as mounds surrounded by ditches and fossilized tree stumps on the sea floor.

Much has been done by academics from the University of St Andrews, and the experts are gathering: climatologists, archaeologists and geophysicists. Dr Richard Bates from that university told *The Daily Mail*:

> Through a lot of new data from oil and gas companies, we're able to give form to the landscape – and make sense of the mammoths found out here, and the reindeer. We're able to understand the types of people who were there.

The traditional view is that the cliff coast came as what we call Doggerland, and was submerged; after that ice age freeze came a rise in temperature, and about 6,000 years ago, the huge increase in heat forced sea levels to rise. Ice sheets had held the land down, and as the water melted, the land rose, much as we see in peat when it absorbs water compared with when it dries. The low-level settlements went down under the water, and these were the first communities lost to the sea. This cannot have been a sudden event; settlements along the Doggerland bridge must have tried to combat the sea, as their descendants were to try to do through the years. Doggerland appears to have finally been lost under water about 7,000 years ago.

There is also the further consideration of the sea bed and the coast itself: the nature of sand, and how that may be itself the instrument of smothering and eradicating homes and villages. The Doggerland settlements may well come into this category, and if we wish to see an example nearer to our own time, then the archaeology done at Kenfig on the coast of South Wales, is available. The *Time Team* crew did some work there. Sand is just as destructive as wind or water, of course. There was a settlement in the Bronze Age at Kenfig, and by the thirteenth century, the sand was beginning to cover everything manmade. Eventually, the church there was moved and relocated to Pyle. What is left at Kenfig, where there once was a castle, is an area of deep sand dunes; when *Time Team* arrived and set to work in 2012, they soon discovered how heavy and awkward a sandy surface was when compared to soil.

Sand has received plenty of attention from scientists, and Anthony Woodward, in an essay on coastal sand, explains what happens to make sand a force to cover and smother:

> Coastal dunes form inland of exposed, sandy beaches, where the strand is wide enough for the sand to dry sufficiently between tides to be blown ashore. Some minor obstacle ... causes wind-blown sand to deposit on its leeward side due to the pocket of slower moving air there. The collected sand gradually accumulates.

In Yorkshire and East Anglia, the sand is blown into ridges. In some places, such as Mablethorpe in Lincolnshire, for instance, it is obvious that the blown sand has been mixed with grass roots, and there is a line of thought that the use of marram grass will help to reduce coastal erosion. But history teaches us that sand can choke whole communities, such as in the case of Culbin, in Scotland, which was entirely covered in the so-called Great Sand Drift of 1694. This horrendous natural disaster forced people from their homes and farms, and as Steven McKenzie wrote in a feature on the catastrophe, 'transformed a once fertile, grain-growing area into a desert.' In the area in question, for the present purpose, sand is a feature of the Holderness river shore. For the smugglers of past times, these sand dunes were ideal places to hide stolen goods.

Doggerland, then, is the first on my list of lost communities. Although we know it only superficially, and through things rather than documents, it is becoming as approachable as a phase in history with its own distinctive people, as any other designated 'period'.

In contrast, there was now a different coast: it was one of chalk cliffs. The Yorkshire coast became a composition of various kinds of clay, with calcareous grit above; accumulated also in these rocks are beds of flint. The whole appeal of the cliffs today reflects this composition. Walking on Filey beach, for instance, south of the Brigg, one sees layers of clay richly filled with everything we expect in sedimentary deposits, from fossils such as ammonites to flint arrowheads. But there are surprises, too: between Hole Bight and Long Bight, close to Saltwick, stegosaur footprints have been found. The comment on this made by the writers of the Geologists' Association guide to the area reminds us that nothing escapes the greed of the sea:

> The prints were made in a red, iron-rich silt ... and were infilled with medium-grain sand. ... As the silt withers away it leaves the sandstone-filled prints in high relief. ... The footprint trail leads in a line heading straight for Whitby Pier. It consists of at least eight prints ... Recent studies of the prints suggest that they were made by a stegosaur.

The authors add, 'Take care not to damage this block; it is already suffering some sea erosion.'

In the centuries before the first Roman landings of Caesar in 55 BC, these various people left their imprint. In a heritage project on this coast done in 2008 by a group from Humber Field Archaeology, their report stated: 'Records of some 17,000 archaeological sites in the East Riding are held by the Humber Sites and Monuments Record in a publicly accessible archive; of these, over 2,000 individual records relate to the Coastal Zone.'

Before my history of the more recent times begins, it is useful to survey what evidence there is of communities further back. In the Humber Field Archaeology project, with reference to that huge and rapid sea level rise in about 6,000 BC, it is clear that this earliest evidence of human presence is abundant now. These Doggerland peoples were hunter-gatherers, and they would have had small settlements that are now out there, beneath the waves. Archaeologists agree that people must have begun to come back to the area in the Late Devensian epoch (about 10,000 BC), before that great ice advance and temperature rise.

By the late Neolithic, the wetlands and meres of Holderness were occupied again by humans; at some point after this, the Anglo-Saxons arrived from Europe. Regarding this early period AD, the historian's task has been made easier by the publication of some broader studies that have given us a clearer impression of what might be called the North Sea Basin. Michael Pye, in *The Edge of the World* (2014), has shifted the focus away from the British coast and looked at Holland and further north. His investigation of land lost to the sea concentrates on Domburg, and the 1647 discovery there of a sunken community. He writes, 'High winds tore up the dunes and made the sea wild in the first days of January 1647. The sand was forced out of the way to show something in the subsoil that should never have been there.' Early human habitations had been revealed, making the world look again at what had been once above the sea level, a place full of living, working people just like the Hollanders of 1647.

This broader view, which looks at the different ways in which countries have coped with loss of coastal land, and how they have tried to understand the lost places, shows just how much the British loss of land has been almost ignored up until now, with only occasional investigations taking place. But the curiosity about later times – the Roman, in particular – has always been there, in the ranks of the antiquaries and historians long before archaeology emerged as a defined profession.

The nature of the lost land has been the subject of enquiry for many centuries. In 1912, Thomas Sheppard, whose book on the lost towns is the main source of information today, used a range of contacts and printed sources to try to measure the lost land. He quotes the chronicle of the abbey of Meaux (pronounced *muce*) in Holderness, and there he finds a record of loss:

> An early record of the loss of land in South-East Yorkshire occurs in the *Meaux Chronicle*. In this, reference is made to a suit for refusal to pay rent on 33 acres of grassland in Orwythfleet, which were carried away by the waters of the Humber between 1310 and 1339. Orwythfleet was apparently on the Humber shore to the west of Easington.

The fourteenth century was the period when land was lost on a grand scale. More particularly, as will be seen in more detail in chapter 5, when the loss of Ravenser is recalled, the middle decades of that century was the time when the most destructive seas were active and widespread destruction followed.

A useful guide to exactly what has been lost is the material relating to the Royal Commission of 1911. One note on Skipsea gives some kind of guide figure:

> The Commissioners are also owners of a farm at Skipsea, having a frontage of about 40 chains to the sea [a chain being just over 66 feet], and on the re-letting in 1890, a reduction of 5½ acres was made in respect of land lost by the encroachment of the sea.

According to Thomas Sheppard in 1912, calculations had been made about the extent of loss of land, over periods recent to him at the time of his writing. For instance, he notes, referring to Easington, how loss may be understood with reference to the information given in the Domesday survey of 1086. Sheppard works out the acreage there in Domesday as being 2,400. He states that there was a loss of 2,100 acres between Domesday and 1800. He gives a more dramatic instance from the same village to back this up:

In 1831, John Field surveyed Ten Chain Close, Easington, which had a frontage to the sea of about half a mile, and it was found that in the sixty-one years that had elapsed since the enclosure of 1770, a strip 127 yards wide had been washed away, a yearly average of over 2 yards.

Locals in Easington obviously had a special interest in the subject of land loss. Sheppard notes that Mount Pleasant Cottage, which had been built in 1876, had a stone made saying that it was 616 yards from the sea. He adds, 'The lettering on this stone is now almost obliterated.' That was just forty-six years after the stone was placed on the cottage. The owner of the place in 1912 told Sheppard that it was then just 470 yards from the sea. Land was being lost at the rate of 4 yards a year.

Modern estimates of loss tend to agree that the coast at Holderness is disappearing at a rate of almost 7 feet every year. The North Sea coast has lost more than 3 miles since the Roman occupation. As far as the geology is concerned, Nick Crane, TV expert on the British coast, sums up what appears to be the process: 'The North Sea is bent on pushing the land back to a line of chalk cliffs which existed 2 million years ago along the eastern edge of the Yorkshire Wolds.'

The period of Roman settlement is of interest in this survey too, because archaeology is busy looking into the kind of presence the Romans had along the coast. By the 70s AD, a few decades after Claudius's successful large-scale invasion of AD 43, the IX Legion had initially led the advance north and had been based in York. At the same time, Roman sea power was being established, and they had a fleet known as the *Classis Britannica*, which was probably based in Dover but must have had some power in the north, as sea power always backs up invasion tactics. Vessels would always use bays and estuaries, and the Humber and Tees were perfect for this. If one looks at the headlands between Scarborough and the Humber, then it is clear that there were a number of places where the Roman fleet would have been based, or their ships would have stayed here when en route for elsewhere.

The map of Britannia by the Roman geographer Ptolemy in the first century AD shows how little was known about the North Sea. On this map, for instance, Scotland is shown as projecting acutely to the east. Along what was later to be Yorkshire, he noted three coastal locations of importance to the Empire: *Dunum*

Bay, *Ganrantuicorum Bay* and *Ocellum Promontorium*. The latter is discussed later when Spurn is described. But the limits of the Roman knowledge are explained by one historian with an eye to practicalities in cartography: 'All of a sudden, the Roman geographer loses all his land data and has to rely on pilots' accounts, with choppy seas and strong currents accounting for the bad data.'

In the Edwardian years, historians knew that there were a great number of Roman remains to be found in scattered places across the county. Discovery was piecemeal and largely done by amateur antiquaries, but nevertheless, there were significant finds, such as villas, pavements, hypocausts. There has been a villa found near Driffield, and on the coast, coins and pottery are continually turning up.

Archaeology has been busy for some time trying to locate these bases. Many of the small Yorkshire coast villages have produced Roman finds, but evidence of actual naval ports is sparse. But it seems likely that Scarborough was such a port, and there has always been an argument that on Filey Brigg, the long headland stretching out on the north of Filey Bay, there was a Roman quay. Michael Fearon, in his history of Filey, has no doubt that there were signal stations there, and he describes the discovery back in 1857:

> The Rev Richard Brooke, the then owner of Carr Naze, arranged for an examination of the site to take place and this revealed walls of large stones with tooled surfaces set in mortar.... Within the walls were five large stones arranged as the corners of a square of size about 60 feet long by 25 feet wide, with one stone at the centre. It is generally accepted that these stones formed the bases for pillars on which rested a superstructure which supported a beacon.

John Ruston, tackling the question of a Roman port at Scarborough, reasons convincingly:

> Scarborough is only 40 miles south of the river Tees and 50 miles north of the river Humber. Second-century pottery and roof tile, found along the Roman road called the 'stony causeway' at Scarborough, has revised the opinion that the road existed to reach the fourth-century signal station on Scarborough rock.

Certainly, there was a full communication network in Yorkshire created by the Roman army. Governor Agricola later made a road called Stanegate, stretching from Carlisle to Corbridge, and then there were camps in North Yorkshire. A main community was established at Aldborough, and many villas have been located around the Vale of York. It seems impossible that, at least by the last decade of the first century AD, there would be no naval network on the coast as advances were made northwards, particularly in the Humber, where there was easy river access from the sea. At Brough, the Roman presence has been established, and there will surely be further finds.

Look at a map of the Yorkshire coast today, going north to south, from Mappleton a little south of Bridlington, down to Kilnsea, and all the hints and indications concerning the historical experience of these encroachments and settlements are there. Off Cowden Sands there is a marked danger area; from Aldbrough Cliff down to Grimston Garth, the cliffs are raw – bare to the sea. Further south, past Tunstall to the Coastguard base, it is the same. At Withernsea, the groynes (there on many old photos) are constantly worked on and strengthened. Further down, all along to Dimlington, there is no coast protection. Finally, at Dimlington, there is the North Sea gas terminal, and driving through this, along the coast road today, the traveller seems to have wandered into some science fiction scenario. Somewhere behind those towers and installations, there is cliff protection. There has to be.

Between Withernsea and Dimlington, there are traces of the former villages. Many are still more or less the place names of previous centuries, but much of their former land has gone. Then we reach Kilnsea, with its long and strengthened banks, but the clay still dissolves and the winds and waves do their work of destruction daily.

A map like this is simply a tag – something pointing to a depth of multi-layered former habitations. Every time the visitor arrives and inspects the cliffs and the sands, there are vestiges of what was there. On rare occasions, such items as Roman brooches have been found, but more often the find will be plastic or tin, cast-offs from today's transitory movements by sea.

How may we begin to understand this invisible history? That is what it is. Shepherd, in 1912, helpfully provided a map showing the places lost. Their names have the sad poetry of an elegy: Orwithfleet, Tharlesthorpe,

Old Kilnsea, and so many more. One way is to take a small-scale example –
Atwick. In a publication of 1891, we have this:

> The parish of Atwick lies on the coast of the German ocean, between
> Skipsea and Hornsea, and contains 2,297 acres of land ... the population
> in 1891 was 298.... Near the centre of the village is an ancient stone
> cross, raised on three steps, which is said to have been, in 1786, 43
> chains from the sea; in consequence of the wasting away of the cliffs it
> is now (1891) less than 38 chains.

In the 2011 Census, the population of the place was 315 and the extent of
the village was given as 2,200 acres. In terms of the population reference, the
word coming to mind is *stasis*: much the same, after 120 years. But in terms
of the land, almost 100 acres have been lost.

In 1891, the listings in the directory tell an interesting story. There was
a carrier to Hull twice a week; post arrived every weekday at 8.25 am, with
the boot maker also running the post provision, and the vicar was Reverend
Edward Gordon. There were a dozen farmers, a blacksmith and four coble
dealers (cobles being the local fishing craft). The school must have been tiny,
and it was run by William Nancarrow.

In my surveys of the villages and towns along this coast, made in early
2016, I found that essentially, there had been very little change in identity
in most places that actually front the sea. In those places where tourism
continues to thrive, there is a determined effort to protect and survive when
it comes to the sea front. But what is still the case today, and has always
been so, is that protection against erosion is only provided where there is
a high level of essential preservation required – usually for industrial or
commercial reasons.

What about the nature of erosion itself? The word signifies so much and
yet the first thought we have on thinking about coastal erosion is that the
sea tides arrive, and driven by wind and tidal surge, batter the cliffs at a low
level, loosening, in the case of the Yorkshire coast, the clay layers and other
vulnerable rock such as grits. This forms an undercutting action, and so
the weight of the cliff above the open gap created begins to crumble. This
does happen, but also the frequency of storms has a dramatic effect, too.

If we put together the elements of geological change, sea levels rising and the tidal action, then it may be seen just how much more may act on the coastal rock.

The key feature of erosion in this concept is longshore drift, and this will be mentioned again later. But it is useful to have an explanation at this point. The Hull Geological Society, on their online feature on the Yorkshire coast, explain this:

> On a wide sandy beach that faces the direction of the incoming waves sand will tend to be pushed up the beach reinforcing its profile; this high beach will then force waves to break offshore before they reach the cliffs. If such a beach is maintained throughout the constant supply of sediment, no further erosion will occur. However, on frontages at a less stable angle, sand will be drawn away, exposing clay surfaces and allowing them to erode. The long-term result of this sensitivity to cliff line orientation is that the whole coast is gradually attempting to develop a shape that lies at right-angles to the predominant north-easterly wave direction.

It is that wind direction that causes the lash of the waves, and also collects pebbles and grit in the backwash. To put it as simply as possible, forces work to take protective sand away, and rock is exposed. That rock on this coast is clay – mud and sedimentary till. My comments on Filey in the introduction explain just how vulnerable this is.

Today, professionals are busy trying to measure and report on the land loss. In 2012, Martin Wainwright wrote about one team at work at a location south of Bridlington. He summarized:

> Using a backpack satnav that plots their course, the team are surveying the current 'last of Yorkshire' and comparing it with where the county ended a year ago. The results vary but in places the county has lost a startling 7m (22 feet) compared to an annual average of 1.7m (5.5 feet).

The rate of erosion has been measured (or at least estimated) by the Hull Geological Society. At Wilsthorpe, just south of Bridlington, they reckon that the erosion rate is 0.43 metres per year; at the south of Easington, down close to Spurn, the rate per year is 1.48 metres.

As the following chapters trace the lost history, it helps to put earlier efforts to stay the concession of land if we look at what legislation exists and what is being done generally. Key was the Coast Protection Act of 1949, and its statement of intention hints at its limitations:

> An Act to amend the law relating to the protection of the coast of Great Britain against erosion and encroachment by the sea; to provide for the restriction and removal of works detrimental to navigation; to transfer the management of Crown foreshore from the Minister of Transport to the Commissioners of Crown Lands.

Unfortunately, in the Act, the word 'may' is used too often. For example:

> The Minister may, where it appears to him expedient for the protection of the land in any area, make an order providing for the constitution of a board, to be known as a coast protection board, which shall be the coast protection authority for that area.

When it comes to practical matters, we have, 'A coast protection authority may acquire', and 'An order made under this section may ...'

For decades, this has been an asset of resolutions that in the end protect only what is financed; the actual provisions of protection relate to a hierarchy of needs, and it looks as though the couples living on the cliffs at Aldbrough today, for instance, have never been assisted and they are clearly very low down on the list of priorities.

There is plenty of monitoring going on, but that is something else, and social history shows that there have always been good intentions from political bases, regional and national. For instance, there is now a Regional Coastline Monitoring Programme, and a coastal handbook has been produced by the Environment Agency and the maritime local authorities. One statement in the handbook sums up what has always been the case, through history: 'Although dynamic beach management solutions are common requiring good quality management data, they are usually limited to capital recharge.... Population centres are spread and there are many areas of coast front farmland or areas of low population.'

The conclusion is that the subject is handled *ad hoc*, and with only a pragmatic approach. This is in spite of this very important admission of the state of affairs in the same handbook: 'Since its creation, this coast has suffered a well recorded history of rapid cliff and foreshore erosion as coastal processes driven by storm seas eat into this relatively soft landmass.' Still, there are some exceptions – places where steps have been taken, as at Mappleton in 1991, when a few million pounds were spent on rock groynes and other rock-built protective belts.

The question arises: what help is there for more knowledge (and future understanding) of the traces of lost communities here, with the help of new technology such as geophysical mapping? This does seem to be where the future work lies. The Yorkshire Coast RCZAS National Mapping Programme project in 2013 has shown some interesting results, most strikingly in such items as an image of alum works off the coast of Kettleness. The overall summary of results was that, in the inter-tidal zone from Whitby down to Donna Nook in Lincolnshire, the survey found more than 1,000 features, including Neolithic sites and square barrows, but also Roman boundary systems. The latter could mean minor roads, as the Romans built many of them, and we tend to only know the main ones by name.

For Roman remains, the most interesting for present concerns is an earthwork signal station at Lythe, in Goldsborough. Other than that, the only other significant Roman site noted was the South Shields Roman fort.

This project also looked at erosion rates, and the most startling was that from 1945 to 1984: at Mappleton, there was a loss of 115 metres. Most tantalizing, with the Yorkshire coast in mind, is the finding at Easington of 'a moated manor and medieval settlement'. The comment on the clarity of what was seen is helpful: 'Some of these earthwork remains appear to be visible on air photographs but were too dispersed and fragmentary in nature to be depicted in mapping. Even so, they were recorded ... to help further investigations.'

As the following chapters will show, such commentary and monitoring have always been done in one way or another, and the hope is that more geophysical work will be done.

Chapter 2

Port Mulgrave to Ravenscar

You gentlemen of England
Who live at home at ease,
How little do you think
Of the dangers of the seas?

Martin Parker, *The Valiant Sailors*

In 2011, a coffee table book was published that featured the Yorkshire coast, and the publishers gave it the title *The Edge of Heaven*. The photographs are wonderful, and the collection of essays is largely descriptive, sometimes elegiac, and always drenched in the sense of awe that the coast gives visitors. One contribution stands out as being closely and engagingly about a lost community, though the remnants are still there to see. The subject is Port Mulgrave, close to Whitby, and the author was David Joy. His essay is headed 'The Lost Port'. The close of the essay sums up the special attraction, bittersweet, of the towns and villages in North Yorkshire facing the wrath of the sea, and he compares the scene today with that of his childhood visit: 'Today, over forty years later, the harbour has been virtually swept away but the area is probably busier than ever. More and more walkers pound the Cleveland Way along the cliff top.'

That cliff top is now dangerous, after a landslip. In a report in the *Gazette and Herald* for August 2016, the author noted that 'access to the actual port area is by a steep and often muddy path. There is no road and no formal pathway down to the harbour … no houses have been built near the shoreline.' This piece is a perfect instance of the value of family history, as the author had found out that his brother had lived in a clifftop house and he had kept a coble. He makes the point that older reference works 'omit it entirely, but David Joy, in *The Edge of Heaven*, has explained Port Mulgrave's industrial history.

That might seem an odd thing to write – thinking of 'industry' in such an awesomely stormy and vulnerable place – but there was industry here, and that was down to a Victorian MP and entrepreneur called Sir Charles Palmer. His country house was at Grinkle Park (now a hotel), but in the 1850s, iron was being worked here. Palmer spent the huge sum of £40,000 on building a railway and digging a mile-long tunnel. The rights for this extraction were bought from the Earl of Mulgrave, whose estates were nearby.

The alum works in North Yorkshire went back a long way. The man responsible for its beginnings was Sir Thomas Chaloner, who, after doing his European grand tour in 1580–84, caught the scientific and entrepreneurial spirit and became convinced that there was alum on his Guisborough estate. He went so far as to bring in Italian workers to do the labouring. The story handed down is that these workers had to be hidden in casks, and even then, when work began, he met problems. These are explained by R. V. Taylor, the Victorian biographer:

> When he had got the mines and works into thorough working order, King Charles I, at the instigation of some of his rapacious courtiers, made a claim to them, as Crown property, and he was compelled to surrender them. They were then let to Sir Paul Pindar at a rent of £12,500 per annum and to the Earl of Mulgrave.

There was still a Mulgrave connection 200 years later.

David Joy explains the workings: 'At each high tide the port became a hive of feverish activity as ore was tipped from the gantry into sailing barges, which were soon conveying 3,000 tons per week to the Palmer shipbuilding and iron furnaces at Jarrow.' Joy adds, 'The miners were not universally revered' and there seems to have been a level of violent hatred of visitors from the works. Their houses are still there, but this is indeed a lost community. The sea is doing its best, along with the ice-cold winds, to lash the place into submission.

The author of the piece in the *Gazette and Herald* found out that his grandfather was an iron worker, and he gives the result of his research:

For many years we thought that our grandparental ancestors lived at Rosedale.... Granddad walked from Rosedale to Skinngrove for his job.... However, the diligent efforts of my brother have revealed that this particular Rosedale was part of Port Mulgrave, a long way from the moorland village of the same name.

The Port was doing well in the mid-century: a report in *The Yorkshire Gazette* for 1859 shows that the cluster of mines around Port Mulgrave – Staithes Belmont, Whitby and Rosedale – together produced 101,425 tons of iron ore. Just a year after this there was a new blast furnace at Jarrow, and at the time it was the largest in the country. One press report explained:

> The iron and limestone will be brought from the Cleveland and Whitby districts by the iron screw steamers which carry coals from Tyne to London. The steamers, having discharged their cargo of coals on the Thames, call on their return northwards at Port Mulgrave.... They are unloaded on the Tyne in front of the new furnaces.

Everything had been worked out smoothly and efficiently.

In 1938, in a press feature, a survey was reported on the number and condition of so-called 'Ghosts of lost ports', and Port Mulgrave was included, with this description from that time:

> A tiny basin sheltered at the foot of precipitous cliffs on a Yorkshire bay near Whitby ... now a ruin of cracking concrete, rotting beams and rusting iron.... The ironstone mines are derelict and a gaping hole in the face of the cliffs is the evidence of a deserted tunnel.

Port Mulgrave did have its part in a notable murder story of 1860. This happened at Winlaton, where a man called John Baty had been killed. The local paper described his body at the inquest as 'battered about the face and in that respect looks like a worn-out pugilist.' He had been out drinking with a notorious character called Thomas Smith, and they had, so Smith claimed later, had a fistfight. The true motive appears to have been robbery, and that was done very brutally. But Smith ran off to hide – and he headed for Port Mulgrave.

The press reported on this:

There are extensive iron mines at Port Mulgrave.... He had got work at the mines.... Port Mulgrave is a lonely, out-of-the-way place, more than 150 miles from the scene of the murder; iron miners are a very distinct race from coal miners and Smith had not chosen a bad retreat.

He was eventually taken by two civilians to Redcar, and Smith's fate was the gallows, after conviction at Durham Assizes in December 1860.

Crime often brings to light the real nature of a place, and gives a rare insight into social history – an insight that is perhaps not available in any other way. Through Smith's story we learn just how isolated and rough Port Mulgrave was. Clearly, it was the very place to go when a man needed to fade into the very dark background.

In 1939, when Ella Pontefract and Marie Hartley toured Yorkshire, they wrote of Robin Hood's Bay: 'In the nineteenth century, numbers of ships were owned by the people, and a big trade was done in exporting coal. Today, there are not enough fishermen in the Bay to man a lifeboat.' The Bay is just 5 miles south of Whitby and 15 miles north of Scarborough. The strange name probably comes from an old tale concerning some French pirates who came into the village to rob, but the mythical hero Robin was there to thwart them, and so came the name. It was settled in the early Middle Ages, in about 1000 by the Vikings, and settlement at the Bay was not notable until around 1536, when the traveller and writer John Leland was there, recording that there were twenty cottages. Not long after that, the number of dwellings grew to fifty.

It is nestling in a fissure between two steep cliffs, and tantalizingly, for little is known of this, some sources say that the manorial courts were held there. In 1540, it was on abbey lands, and at that time it perhaps came under the name North Fyling. Losses continued through the ages, such as the hotel that once stood on Way Foot and had to be replaced after being washed away in 1843. William Page, writing in 1923, wrote that at the time it had the elementary school along with Mamar Dale Beck and Yaddow Mills.

The fishing industry was the main concern, of course, and that did well. But the place has been battered by the sea and the gales, and a number of homes have been lost. As recently at 1950, a cottage fell down into the waves. Sea walls have been built to try to help the situation, the latest one being installed in 2001.

Of the village there now, most of the houses are from a 1914 building programme, and in the lower bay, the dwellings are much earlier, going back to the eighteenth century. It is a place of shipwrecks, smuggling history and also Methodism. The chapel has a story of its own: it is now the Swell café bar but it began life as a chapel, back in 1725, when locals financed the building. The tale goes that when this became a Methodist chapel, completed by 1750, and it expanded, as the swell website notes, 'they acquired Miss Tindale's garden, Mary Cobb's pig cote and James Johnson's blacksmith forge.' It was rebuilt in 1841, and again in 1846.

The chapel is entirely typical of the attempts to dig in and make a living on this coast, which is my central theme: as the website relates, 'records indicate that in 1899 there were further landslips to the rear of the property.... It took a further thirty years to conclude the search for a new property, during which time coastal erosion threatened.' There were people along this coast in the past that are deftly defined as a series of lives clinging to a rock, a phrase once used in conversation with a Jersey historian to describe his own people.

In May 2014, *The Yorkshire Post* ran a feature dealing with the erosion here. Scarborough Council met to consider the problem and *The Yorkshire Post* quoted Jim Dillon, the authority chief executive, as saying, 'The sea wall currently defends forty-four properties that would be lost to erosion within the next 100 years should the sea wall be left to fail.' A grant of £50,000 is on offer from the Environment Agency.

The erosion problems go back a very long way: since the last years of the eighteenth century, 200 properties have gone. *The Yorkshire Post* summed up that the community 'lived in fear of total loss.' Here is the familiar story again: those slippages of the cliffs, which go on relentlessly, cutting into the terrain and reshaping the inlets and bays.

In 1780, there was a mighty landslip that took away twenty-two houses and most of King Street; in 1945, Mrs Florence Skelton was having cup of tea, as one press report has it, 'in her front room, when the back wall disappeared – carried away by a cliff fall. She opened her door to find herself looking out at the North Sea.' Ten years earlier, as *The Nottingham Evening Post* reported, 'The kitchen of Scar Cliff cottage, occupied during the summer by Mr Mather, Todmorden, has gone over the cliff, and the rest of the building is in a precarious condition.' In that year, 1936, there was great concern felt at Robin Hood's Bay by the people living on the road down to the shore; the cliff face had moved. Summer residences were threatened in this instance.

At Regent's Cottage, a Barnsley man, Mr Wilkins, reported there were deep fissures appearing in the path leading to the door. He took out all the furniture, but he was not going to relinquish his place at the Bay: he told the press that he had bought some land higher up and he intended to rebuild his cottage up there.

This was caused, most likely, not by the sea directly, but by heavy rains and then a dry season, causing a soil creep rather like the Scarborough example of Holbeck Hall.

In their educational materials to invite thought about the local problem, the North York Moors National Park Authority presents pictures of sea defences through time: a Victorian high brick wall; a concrete dam wall structure from the 1970s; and a more recent rock revetment. The latter method does seem to be winning favour. Recent visits to the coast by me and others have noticed that the common approach now is to use gabions – netted rock arrangements – after the fashion of military installations such as Camp Bastion. Fittingly, these were invented by a Yorkshireman – Jimi Heselden, from Leeds, who left school at fifteen with no academic qualifications. Today, they seem to be one of the most productive and reliable methods of at least slowing the force of erosion.

Then we have Ravenscar, just 10 miles north of Scarborough. A century ago, some thought that it would rival Bridlington and Scarborough as a principal holiday destination, but this never worked out. Like Filey and Flamborough, it was the site of a Roman signal station. More recently, the site of a Roman fort there was built on by the Beswick family, and later arrived the man who developed the alum works, Captain William Childs. When he died in 1829, his daughter inherited, and here we have a link with one of the Regency's great celebrities: Dr Willis, who treated George III for his porphyria.

Ravenscar's fame rests on alum. This is used as a fixative in dyeing processes, and in the sixteenth century, it was imported from Italy. But when greater historical events meant that this had to stop, there was a need for its production in the domestic market. In stepped Thomas Chaloner, who set up the first ever alum production in Guisborough, North Yorkshire. He saw that the coastal areas had shale, and alum was quarried from this – a flat rock resembling slate.

The drawback in alum production was the time span: it took several months to burn and leach the material, so that aluminium sulphate liquor could be obtained. To this, urine was needed for the final stage. Clearly, this was not an industry with any pleasant working conditions. In 1607, Chaloner had teamed up with Lord Sheffield, who owned the Mulgrave estates (being the Earl of Mulgrave) and the production slowly began. But it was in the nineteenth century that Ravenscar became prominent, along with other places on the coast, and this did not end until 1871.

Along this stretch of coast, there have been some significant case studies in the last twenty years, and many have been documented by the 'Coastview' website (see bibliography), which assembles people's experience of erosion on all the British coasts. The saga of Tony Oliver's home in Robin Hood's Bay was reviewed on the site. Oliver bought a Georgian farmhouse on the cliff, seduced by the vista and the overall environment. But, reported Nick Nuttall:

> Today, his much increased proximity to the waves has proved a nightmare. Erosion and gales are lashing the family from their North Yorkshire home. They wanted to stay, but the elements have proved too powerful and property prices have plummeted. ... Seven years after moving in, Oliver is drawing up an evacuation plan after facing an unequal struggle with the elements battering the cliffs.

Oliver's experience must be that of many, but his case, reported in 1995, it must surely be one of the most vividly described. At one point he saw a river of clay pouring down the cliffs of his home, Stoupe Bank Farm. He told Nick Nuttall that when he bought the house at an auction, there was 'no whisper of a threat' from the sea, which was then 32 metres away. What he wanted to do back then was move the farm further inland but this was refused by the local planning authority.

Strangely, the farm is still there today and is currently for sale (August 2016). Oliver told Nuttall that there was, in 1995, no plan to protect that part of the coast, and although there had been some work done at Robin Hood's Bay itself, he had no protection. He said, 'The economics do not justify a coastal defence scheme here.'

Chapter 3

Scarborough to Flamborough

Thus ornament is but the guilèd shore
To a most dangerous sea.
William Shakespeare, The Merchant of Venice

Between 3 and 5 June 1993, the Holbeck Hall hotel on the Scarborough cliffs slipped down onto the cliff and then, mixed with glacial till of around 1 million tons in weight, it was annihilated. The Holbeck had been built in the year of the great military disaster of Isandlwana in the Zulu War, when Disraeli was running the country – 1879. It had survived everything the Yorkshire weather could throw at it over the following years, and that is a very important point, because the sea was not the cause of the slip.

It was a sight that the locals looked at aghast, as they say in Yorkshire, flummoxed: surely it is not possible for a great strong building like that to just slip away? Passers-by were accustomed to seeing bits of clay slither down into the rubble at the cliff bottoms, and they knew that the North Sea gales could ravage everything in sight, but here was a landmark on the map, a place referred to by everyone, from the postman to the visitors arriving with their suitcases. It might have been called by some a fixture on the landscape, but after sober reflection, when the furore died down, many local people would have placed it in the context of a past time and the long succession of loss and disintegration in their neck of the woods.

The cause was a rotational landslide: the rock was Scalby mudstone and sandstone, and the hotel was built on a low cliff. There were warnings: several weeks before the disaster, there were cracks in the tarmac walkways, and the front garden began to disappear. Guests and staff were evacuated and the downhill creep began. There are numerous reasons why soil on a slope will creep and gradually cause a slide, but none of these are in this instance related to the action of the sea. The owners thought otherwise, and a court case ensued, as the local Council were taken to court, but the action failed.

The event was caught on camera, of course, and so many viewers on TV thought that this was a case of coastal erosion. More likely is the explanation involving water retention of plants' roots on the slope and the water building up in the soil. Whatever the reason, the sea was not the culprit.

Still, the horrendous images of the slide confirmed a persistent feeling of imminent dread when the North Sea was anywhere near. Scarborough, a spa town originally, and now famous for many things, including the Stephen Joseph Theatre and Alan Ayckbourn, has, however, had its battles with the sea.

In the late eighteenth century, the famous playwright Richard Brinsley Sheridan chose to call one of his plays *A Trip to Scarborough*, and in that work he has a local girl in the tale. In Act One, her father and her lifestyle are explained:

Her father, Sir Tunbelly Clumsy, lives within a quarter mile of the place, in a lonely old house, which nobody comes near. She never goes abroad and sees company at home. To prevent misfortunes, she has her breeding within doors. The parson of the parish teaches her to play upon the dulcimer, the clerk to sing, the nurse to dress.

Sheridan chose the town to represent the rural dullness that audiences laughed at then, as opposed to the metropolitan mindset in London. But in reality, Scarborough was far from dull, and at that time its popularity grew immensely.

Scarborough has always been, at least since the eighteenth century, defined as a holiday resort. Writing in the 1930s, Ella Pontefract and Marie Hartley placed it firmly in what they called 'the Middle Coast' of Yorkshire, and they noted how it had been overwhelmed by modernity: 'Then, around the marine drive with its border of waiting cars and buses, you are at the North, where a frenzied life has overtaken the family scene of a generation ago.' Their account picks up on nothing that sees the North Sea as a threat, and there is no reference to anything swallowed up by the water. In contrast to their writing on the lower coast, all is sunny and bright here. Centuries before their visit, medicinal wells had been discovered, and investment followed.

However, all is not so secure. A feature in *The Scarborough News* in March 2014 made the point that expenditure of £24 million is needed if the magnificent Spa Complex and 380 other residences are to be maintained and protected from both heavy seas and the threat of landslides. At that time, there were some voices of dissent regarding the costs involved.

In 1890, the Duke of Clarence visited the town to open a new area of the pleasure gardens and the marine drive. Ironically, with Holbeck Hall in mind, eleven years earlier, as *The Daily Graphic* reported, there had been a natural disaster on a major scale:

> In 1879, a large portion of the south end of the undercliff slipped forward into the sea. The erosion of the base of the cliff by the action of the sea had made great inroads into the cliff, and the Corporation decided to acquire the whole of the undercliff ... and to lay it out as pleasure gardens between the Castle Hill and Peasholm ...and to erect a sea defence at the base with a marine carriage drive.

John Coode devised the whole scheme and the work was to cost £150,000. There was to be no risk involved in the work on the undercliff, as *The Graphic* noted, 'The undercliff, comprising about 25 acres, has been effectually drained, at great cost.' That is the point: investment. It is not hard to envisage what might be the case in a century from now in most of the Yorkshire resorts and smaller communities: erosion at the limits to north and south, and the retention of the central promenades where money has been spent on the sea walls and groynes.

The Royal Commission of 1911 made a special point of noting and describing the Scarborough defences, but made a strangely complacent comment about the coast as a whole:

> The coast of Yorkshire as far south as Flamborough Head is subject to only very slight erosion. The chief places where erosion has occurred proceeding from north to south are as follows: Staithes ... Sandsend,

just to the north of Whitby, Whitby itself; to the north of Scarborough; south of Filey Brigg and within the parish of Muston, just south of Filey.

The erosion may have been considered 'slight' without close inspection. In fact, there were cliff collapses along that coast, and these have continued into modern times.

Ten years before the work on the new pleasure gardens, Thomas Walker wrote to the local paper about a landslip on the North Bay. It had also been noticed that on the Castle Hill, the Ladies Well was 5 yards closer to the cliff edge than it had been eighty years earlier. The North Bay paths are still liable to sink, as is the case at Filey between the cobble landing and the Brigg.

Scarborough, along with Hornsea and Withernsea, lost its pier too. The Promenade Pier was built in 1869 after three years of building work; it was 1,000 feet long, and was designed by Eugene Birch. Tom Rowntree was secretary and manager, and the cost of the work was £15,000. As happened with other piers, the beginning of the end was when a vessel cracked into the structure, and that happened when a yacht, the *Escalpa*, did just that. But it survived the accident and entertainments were planned and performed. The last concert was in 1904. G.J. Mellor, writing in *The Dalesman*, comments on the end of the pier:

> Scarborough's pier suffered from lack of patronage during its lifetime. One reason was that the North Side of those days was hardly developed. ... Had the pier lasted a little longer it might have become a council-owned concern. Now, like the pier, the trams, which did so much to open up the amenities of the North Side, are but a memory.

If people holidaying nearby at Cayton Bay notice landslips, the Scarborough Maritime Heritage Centre explains, 'The cliffs around Cornelian and Cayton areas are just made of soil.' The readers of the 1911 report should have been given simple and straightforward facts such as that, rather than sweeping generalizations.

But the fact remains that in terms of dwellings and communities lost to the North Sea, we need to move further south. Filey, Cayton and Speeton have had their share of horrendous weather, and some of these tales of meteorological disasters help to explain the intensity of destruction on this coast. In 1908, for instance, J.S. Wayne, who was then a schoolboy, kept a record of his visit to Filey. He noted, at the end of August:

> After tea it rained and the wind rose. A great gale raged. Williamson [his landlady's husband] was out between Whitby and Scarborough. His wife, Anna, said, 'I do feel anxious for him. I wish it was morning.' This was not a 'half-penny paper panic' but deep and grounded fear. We had never heard the wind so loud.

On 3 September, the boy noted, 'We extended our ... walk so as to look at our 1902 lodgings, in which we heard of the Speeton disaster that summer.'

This refers to the loss of the *Tynemouth*, a steam trawler from Grimsby, close by Bempton Cliffs on 12 April 1902. All crew members were lost, and she had been seen by a coble moving very close to the Filey Brigg, and then she ran aground. The Bempton Cliffs, now a bird study reserve, have treacherous waters close by. A lifeboat went out but wasn't able to save anybody, and later the bodies of the seamen were washed up on shore.

Speeton was at one time owned by the Augustinian priory at Bridlington; in 1290, the priory was given control of the 'free warren' of the area, and so they had a lot of land, and some of that has gone. There was a chaplain named in the parish in 1451, and clearly the place thrived for a very long time.

The chapel at Speeton is of particular interest – a small parish church dedicated to St Leonard. One of its most notable visitors was Charlotte Brontë, who called there in 1852, and she wrote:

> On Sunday afternoon I went to a church which I should like Mr Nicholls to see [he was her future husband]. It was certainly not more than thrice the length and breadth of our passage, floored with brick, the walls green with mould, the pews painted white, but the paint almost worn off with time and decay. At one end there is a little gallery for the singers, and when these personages stood up to perform, they all turned

their backs upon the pulpit and parson. The effect of this manoeuvre was so ludicrous I could hardly help laughing.

Also at Speeton, near the Bempton Cliffs, there has been a find known now as the 'Dulcey Dock'. This was a manmade brick dock at the bottom of the cliffs at Speeton, and it appears to have been made in the late nineteenth century. The accepted story behind it is that a Humber keel, named *Dulcey*, used to work the route between Speeton and Hessle, just a little west of Hull. It is a very dangerous area to navigate and wrecks are well documented, notably that of a trawler called *Skegness*, which was smashed in September 1935.

Local recollection says that part of Dulcey Dock could still be seen (and played on by children) in the 1930s. It seems that the trading route down to Hessle involved the production of chalk whiting, and for a long period the steps of the dock were maintained, but only to create a rock pool for swimming. Ces Mowthorpe, writing a personal memoir of the dock, recalled:

> During the summers of 1944–45, training was carried out with two Browning machine guns on mountings, almost where the RSPB visitor centre is today. These were serviced by a Sergeant Armourer and seven airmen who 'lived out' under canvas close by. As an ATC cadet, the writer fired these guns several times at drogues towed across the bay … whilst waiting around I was horrified to see a young airman running up the aforementioned steps.

Filey itself, formed of the soft boulder clay, which runs between the solid Brigg down to the tough chalk of Flamborough, has a history in respect of its coping with the sea very much like that of Scarborough to the north. Michael Fearon, historian and former curator of the museum at Filey, explained in his history of the town:

> In earlier years there had been constructed sea defence works, particularly between Carr Gate Hill and Crescent Hill. … That there were those prepared to build such impressive buildings as the Ackworth and Downcliff so close to the water with so little defence is a matter of

some surprise. However, by the late 1880s, it was clear to many that a major work was increasingly necessary.

By 1893, the work was begun: a string sea wall and promenade were underway, and as Michael Fearon notes, 'The number of men employed was more than 200. ... It was calculated that 40,000 cubic yards of material were used to infill behind the wall.'

The history of the stretch of coast from Scarborough to Flamborough is one that embraces plenty of dramatic events, mainly caused by extreme weather; there has been an ongoing struggle with the sea along that coast, but no recent community is known to be under the sea there. However, in spite of the 1890s' sea wall, as the 1911 report on erosion quoted earlier states, 'So far as can be ascertained, the protective works undertaken by this council have not produced any effect on the neighbouring coast, and no defensive measures have been adopted in the districts adjoining.' In desperation, south of the Brigg, individual property owners in the late Victorian and Edwardian years built their own wooden barriers.

The 'lost' settlement here has to be the Roman one, and that is a continuing enquiry. Michael Fearon noted in his history that myths and oral tradition were creeping into general knowledge in the area. He writes: 'There is ... nothing to substantiate legends associating the Emperor's bath, a large rock pool on the Brigg, with the Emperor Constantine.'

However, there is the question of the jetty, known as the 'spittal', which juts out at an angle from the Brigg rocks. In 1972, there was an underwater search of the location, but it had no definite results. The pier or jetty is 180 metres long and 7 metres wide. Thomas Sheppard, inspecting this in 1922, considered it to be manmade, but other opinions disagree. In 1997, the Filey Brigg Research Group did a study and their conclusions were that the rocks are probably manmade: 'It is difficult to visualize what natural processes could give rise to a structure with such steep sides and homogeneous construction. It is totally different from any other part of the Brigg.' They then add, with reference to medieval piers at other places, 'These piers were constructed of a stone core around timber planks and a top decking. ... this method of construction being very common until the 1900s.'

It seems more than likely that we have a medieval jetty here, and that at a lower level, across Filey Bay, there may well be other evidences of human habitation.

Chapter 4

From Bridlington to Out Newton

The dragon-green, the luminous, the dark,
The serpent-haunted sea.
                    James Elroy Flecker, *The Gates of Damascus*

We owe so much to Thomas Sheppard, and his maps are always there, comfortingly reassuring the modern reader or writer as efforts are made to check exactly what *was*, and what still *is*. He listed all the little hamlets, giving due attention to their place in his annals of defeat along this beautiful coast. He was a geologist with an antiquarian bent and he saw the wider picture. He will be my guide through these chapters, and without him, there would be no track to follow in searching out the fields and stones eaten away as surely as the clock ticks and time passes.

On Sheppard's map showing the coast from Bridlington to Out Newton, there are twenty settlements he locates in the area between the current and the Roman coastline. To look systematically at every one of these would be to see a pattern repeated, and so some representative places have been selected. The two largest locations in that stretch of coast are Hornsea and Withernsea, and their story will follow, but first, a look at an entirely typical lost community will create a template for what comes later. This is Aldbrough.

In early 2015, Tony Francis visited the village, to write a feature called 'Terra non firma' for *The Dalesman*. He interviewed Kathy Bartle, who had bought a cottage on the cliffs there in 1988, moving from Sheffield. This is the situation, as described by Tony Francis: 'A mere 37 metres of so-called terra firma separate Cedar Cottage from the deep. Seaside Road plunges off the edge of the world.' The significant point, with regard to the current history, is the knowledge of land now gone: 'They also remember an amusement arcade, a car park and a toilet block – all claimed by the sea.'

There is a dramatic contrast here too, and this is replicated in so many places: Aldbrough number two, down the road, is fine, thanks; not under threat. As Tony Francis explains, 'I'd go so far as to say it's a split village – us and them. The sane and the insane. Period four-bedroom houses near the centre still fetch £400,000.'

In 1891, the information in the directories is hard headed. This is typified by a statement concerning Aldbrough's most celebrated historical tale – that of Ulf, a Saxon thane. This little note, on St Bartholomew's church, is significant:

> Built into the wall of the south aisle is the circular stone of a sun dial ... around the margin, in Saxon characters, is inscribed, 'Ulf raised this church for Hanum's and for Gunthard's souls.' The phraseology and the eight divisions of the day clearly show that the dial belongs to a time anterior to the Conquest ... and it is also equally certain that it does not now occupy its original position. But whether the church that Ulf erected stood, as some writers assert, 'in the vicinity of the castle, near the shore', and was long ago submerged by the sea, is open to doubt.

At the time, considerations of what was lost to the sea were perhaps of less importance than the established facts. Early history was, one infers, left to the geologists and antiquaries.

In 1891, Aldbrough had a population of 666 people; it comprised 4,913 acres, and was a thriving place generally, with reasonably good communications with Hull and elsewhere. It had the Royal Hotel, and several shopkeepers and craftspeople. But parts of it had been lost. The writer of the directory notes, 'The castle is supposed to have been washed away by the sea many centuries ago.' There is some doubt about that, as in spite of a reference to finance supplied by Stephen, Earl of Albemarle, in 1115 to have a church established, some think that this is a confusion, with the castle in question being that of Skipsea, not far away.

The village had certainly shrunk over the century; in 1823, the population was 998. That fall in numbers is being repeated today, as census figures show. The villages clustered around Aldbrough have also receded; Ringborough, for example, by 1850, was only one farm. The fate of the land that has been lost at Aldbrough and at neighbouring places is powerfully understood with a look at Thomas Jefferys' map of the area printed in 1772. This map, put alongside the ordnance survey of 1854, shows Great Colden. Between those two dates, lost to the sea are: the Green manor house, the Cross Keys pub, a Methodist chapel and two lime kilns, to say nothing of twenty-two fields. The cliff recession had been 292 metres. As the entry in the British History Online account of the village shows, there was a beer house near the sea in 1832, and in 1836, Robert Raikes began to build what became the Talbot Hotel. Since 1885, the Talbot, the Spa Inn and the Royal Hotel have been lost.

Just a few miles south of Bridlington, a cluster of villages lie – or have lain – in vulnerable positions, north of Skipsea. Their situation was noticed and assessed in the 1911 report on coastal erosion. These are Wilsthorpe, Auburn and Fraisthorpe, and they provide a rare example of one man's investment in trying to save them. This was Sir Charles Strickland of Boynton Hall. The 1911 Royal Commission report assured readers that Sir Charles had certainly done his best to protect his shores:

Four groynes were erected by Sir Charles Strickland about 1892–94. Their skeletons still remain. They did very little, if any, good, even temporarily, for the sea soon got behind them. The only sort of groynes that would be of any use … would be long low groynes gradually raised at and just above low water mark. Whether they would be worth their cost is another question.

Strickland did his best, and he had quite a challenge, as the report states that the Wilsthorpe cliffs had eroded more quickly after some sea walls were made at Hilderthorpe. The author of the report had clearly been in the area and talked to people, rather than sitting in a London office, because he wrote, 'Fishermen tell me that they can now feel the "rebound" from the walls well out to sea as far south as Auburn, and this rebound probably tells on the cliffs.'

Strickland was the 8th baronet; he was born in 1819 and died in 1909. Some claim that he was the model for the fictional 'Martin' in the classic novel about Rugby school (which he attended), *Tom Brown's Schooldays*. He was certainly a presence in North Yorkshire: as well as trying to save his land, he was also a judge on the northern circuit assizes, and High Sheriff of Yorkshire in 1880.

His Wilsthorpe area was vulnerable to the tides; there is no doubt of that. The 1911 report notes: 'At Wilsthorpe, erosion has been going on for many years but until a few years ago the cliff was not going at an appreciable rate south of the spot marked.' This refers to their map of the coast, which shows past and present coastlines. As a recent archaeological survey comments, 'Wilsthorpe consists of sunken pathways, fields, a pond, hollows, earthwork banks and ditches, marking the western and southern limits of a formerly more extensive settlement, now lost to the sea; part also lies below modern housing.' As with so many of these places on the coast here, there was once a chapel, and we know that in the late Victorian years it went, because the *Bulmer's Directory* of 1892 states that the place had gone within living memory.

Between Hornsea and Aldbrough lies Cowden, another victim of the sea, and in extreme form. In 1995, Peter Mullen reported on the case of Sue Earle, who had a farm there then. He was told by Sue that 'Topper, our pregnant cow, fell over the cliff when it collapsed.... Astonishingly, she turned up safe and sound 5 miles down the coast. She gave birth with no trouble at all.' Sue's farm was bought by her uncle in the 1950s, and then it was around 60 metres from the cliff; in 1995, it was just a few paces away. Earl explained to Peter Mullen, 'We've had to evacuate buildings. The cliff road used by the farm delivery lorries and holidaymakers was first closed by the authorities and now it has gone right over the cliff.'

A quarter of a mile away, there was a pig farm run by Shawn and Yvonne Mars. Mr Mars told a similar story:

When I bought this farm seven years ago it was 6 acres, but now it's only a bit more than 4. We knew about the coastal erosion when we bought the farm but land was disappearing at 1½ metres a year when we moved in. This year alone, we've lost 15 metres.

Cowden is part of Mappleton, and Little Cowden was a separate parish, but that was claimed by the sea some time during the seventeenth century.

In 1852, the whole parish of Mappleton covered 3,445 acres, and of these, 767 were in Cowden. Shockingly, by1891, just forty years later, it was 3,424 acres. Twenty-one acres lost to the sea is an extensive piece of land, and a consequent loss of a fair amount of income. At its height, in the fourteenth century, the population of Great and Little Cowden together had eighty-six poll tax payers in 1377, falling to just twenty-eight assessed for hearth tax 300 years later. The population figures for more recent times tell a story of decline, in step with the loss of land: both Cowdens together in 1801 had 115 people, and in 1881, the figure was just ninety-five.

If we really need to understand the nature of the coastal town experience through history in this part of the world, then attention turns to Hornsea, around 18 kilometres south of Bridlington. On Thomas Sheppard's map, Hornsea Beck and Hornsea Burton, the lost villages, are indicated.

I visited Hornsea in May 2016, well before the main tourist season. On a cool, windy day, workmen were repairing and boarding the groynes on the northern area of the beach. From the end of the prom, a cabin staffed by coastal management was occupied and busy. It was clear that the long battle with the sea was still going on. There were solid wooden boards being fixed between groynes, making a firm barrier.

Hornsea is mentioned in Domesday and was then a port. The directory of 1891 was written at the time when the revolution of the railway had happened:

> A line of railway connecting it with Hull was constructed by the Hull and Hornsea Railway Co in 1864, and three years later, the line was taken over by the NER [North Eastern Railway]. ... Since the opening of this railway, Hornsea has risen to considerable favour as a sea bathing place, and many rows of terraces of good modern houses have been erected for the accommodation of visitors.

In 1912, Sheppard gave a detailed account of the loss of land and buildings around Hornsea. Hornsea Beck and Hornsea Burton, linked to the town, are shown as lost to the sea on Sheppard's map, and the 1891 directory sums up the fate of Hornsey beck:

Many places formerly on the coast of Holderness have been engulfed by the sea. Amongst them is Hornsey Beck, once a hamlet in this parish, the last portion of which was swept away about 150 years ago. There was a pier at the end of Hornsey Beck in the reign of Elizabeth, but it had been destroyed by the sea before 1609, as we learn from an inquisition … Thirty-eight houses and as many little closes joining were decayed by the flowing of the sea.

Thomas Sheppard moves rather closer to the actual details of the places lost, and his pictures also tell a powerful story. He accounts for Hornsea Burton too, with plenty of facts: 'According to Kirby's Inquest in the thirteenth century, the heirs of Gilbert de Mapleton held in Hornsea Burton "6 carucates of land", say 720 acres; in 1852, there were 409 acres, and now there are considerably less.' He also quotes a document from 1609 a rare account of the awareness of land loss: 'We find decayed, by the flowing of the sea, in Hornsea Beck, since 1546, thirty-eight houses … also we find, since the same time, forcibly illustrates the deterioration of property.'

One very clear indication of change due to the sea in Hornsea is the story of the pier. Joseph Armytage Wade was the entrepreneur who did so much to develop Victorian Hornsea. Historian Howard Peach calls him 'The man who made Hornsea' in a feature for the *Yorkshire Journal*. Wade, after quite a struggle, had the pier completed by 1880, but tragically, it was soon after destroyed in a storm. But it was remade, and it survived until 1897. Howard Peach summarizes the story: 'On the night of 28 October, an exceptionally bad storm hurled a ship, the *Earl of Derby*, against the pier head, leaving but 750 feet of the original 1,072. The sad remnant remained in place for many years before demolition.'

The pier was built in 1865, and was the first of the Yorkshire piers. After the damage to the structure, there was, as expert on the county piers G.J. Mellor quoted in the last chapter, 'Litigation … and in the meantime, the remaining portion was subjected to the ravages of the very heavy seas.' At that time, the estimate of land loss was about 4 yards a year, and as Mellor adds, 'An old jingle throws interesting light on the serious effects of this erosion down the years:

If Hornsea steeple, when built were thee
Ten miles off Beverley, ten miles off sea.'

Now that the stage has been reached at which the curious ask, what sort of people and homes, what sort of buildings, went down off Hornsea? The subsoil clay and gravel have been farmed for oats, barley, beans and peas. As with other townships, the centuries brought fairs and markets, and the church had a strong presence, of course. The church there in the Middle Ages was owned by the monks of St Mary's at York, and in 1423, the tithes were taken by that abbey. The town was a port in those early days, and then, by the eighteenth century, Hornsea followed Scarborough and Bridlington in being a place where people took holidays. Charlotte Brontë stayed there for three weeks in 1853, and she also visited Scarborough and Filey.

The special attraction at Hornsea was, and still is, the Mere. The 1891 directory explains the appeal of this:

On the western side of town is Hornsea Mere, the largest sheet of water in the county, and the last of the lakes whose memory is preserved in several place names in Holderness. The surrounding country is flat ... but an abundance of wood on the northern and western margins, and four wooded islands in the lake, compensate not a little for the absence of mountain and crag, and impart to the scene a quiet, picturesque beauty. The Mere is irregular in outline, measuring, from east to west, about 1¾ miles in breadth, and covers an area of 467 acres.

By the nineteen century, as Hornsea looked towards Hull and elsewhere for tourists and day trippers, the work went on, and it was the kind of work that had been undertaken in the lost villages of Burton and Beck. There were eight farmers, including Edward Clayton, of the Old Hall, along with cow keepers, smiths, wheelwrights, and grocers.

Skipsea, a little way to the north, is arguably the most telling and representative of the towns slipping away today. I visited Skipsea in early 2016, and after asking a local where the coast was, I was directed to a caravan site. I went to the cluster of caravans, noticed a small shop and then a club. I walked for 50 yards and came suddenly to a barrier warning of danger. The tarmac road ended dramatically at this barrier. To my left was the club, with a small area beside it near the cliff edge, and to my right, behind a tall mesh fence, was a row of houses perilously close to the edge. A young man was mowing his postage-stamp size front lawn, with the waves raging below, over the precipice. Skipsea is indeed potentially an iconic image for disappearing Yorkshire.

I also asked where the castle was, as this was marked on my map. 'I wouldn't call it a castle ... just a mound,' was the reply. The place is not in Domesday, but is mentioned in 1298, when it is noted that the rector had a tithe of fish there. The castle in question relates to Drogo de Bevere, the first Norman lord of Holderness. His home was at Skipsea Brough, and a description was given in the directory:

It stood upon an artificial mound, 500 yards in circumference, steep and difficult to ascend.... The outworks form a crescent, extending about half a mile.... On top of the mound stood the 'donjon keep' but nothing now remains except a piece of wall.

As so often in such locations, there is a paranormal tale attached to the historical record. Drogo allegedly married the niece of William the Conqueror, but he is supposed to have poisoned her and fled. The tale now told is that she haunts the ruined walls. There is also the legend that the four deep holes in the moat, noticed in Victorian times, came from two brothers fighting, at the time of the Civil War, for their inheritance. They were supposed to have fought all day long and then went down, stabbed, and dying. The places where their feet implanted themselves were alleged to be paranormal, and as the brothers were buried there, later generations moved around the area with a sense of fear.

In the 1890s, Skipsea was ¾ of a mile from the coast; now it lies very much on the edge of land. Archaeological work has been done at Skipsea Withow, which has shown some information about the Neolithic landscape and people there. The report on this explains:

Skipsea Withow shows a well-defined Neolithic clearance phase with cereal pollen and weeds of cultivation, indicating arable farming. The clearance was short-lived and followed by woodland regeneration.... Worked wood, probably coppiced and associated with a track way, has been dated..:. Bronze Age and Iron Age settlement sites associated with the meres, the so-called 'crannogs', are known from the area.

On Thomas Sheppard's map, there is a cluster of lost villages marked, and the 1891 directory explains what these were:

Hythe was a hamlet in this parish, destroyed by the sea before the commencement of the 15th century. It would appear from its name to have been a small port or haven. The abbot and convent of Meaux derived an income of £30 from this place, yearly, from the tithe of fish.

Cleeton was another hamlet that disappeared. At the time of the Domesday survey, *Cletune* was a manor, stated to have been 5 miles in length. It had previously belonged to Harold, and was valued at £32 in Edward the Confessor's time.

Here we come upon one of the outstanding historians with regard to lost villages: Maurice Warwick Beresford (1920–2005). Beresford made a specialism of the search for deserted and lost medieval villages; in 1946, he had an insight that changed his life when he saw that the archaeological site at Bittersby in Leicestershire was once a medieval community. He then went on to locate several deserted villages, using very basic aerial photography, but by the 1970s, when he published his *Deserted Medieval Villages*, a catalogue had emerged, and one of these related to Cleeton.

In 1952, Beresford referred to Cleeton as a 'drowned village'; he had pioneering work by George Poulson to go on (reaching back to 1841). He located the site of Cleeton just off the coast at a spot parallel to the B1242, a few hundred yards north of the spot on the cliffs level with Far Grange Park and the Golf Club. Back in the Domesday years, in the 1080s, Cleeton was the major settlement in the Skipsea area. It included the sokes (areas stipulated in the Danelaw) of Dringhoe and Upton, now also gone. But later its presence was rather eclipsed by records of Skipsea. But the manor of Cleeton was important. In 1338, William de la Pole, a wealthy wool merchant from Hull, was given Cleeton along with Burstwick, Owthorne, Withernsea and Kilnsea.

The manor was in a place called Hall Garth Hill and it appears to have been inhabited between the thirteenth and sixteenth centuries. At its most thriving phase, records show that between seven and thirteen men worked its land. Then, in 2004, the television *Time Team's* historians were at work on Skipsea. This entailed a geophysical survey of an area, suggesting that there might be parts of the medieval Cleeton still under land rather than water. But the matter is not settled yet, and as has been pointed out, the name 'Cleeton' was used to cover a very wide stretch of land, rather than one specific village. Various old maps show conflicting references with regard to place names of farms and other places, and so today, Sheppard's location of Cleeton as being washed away is not definitely challenged.

As for William de la Pole, he will appear again in this book, as he was possibly from a Ravenser family, but also had Hull connections. Ravenser figures very prominently in the later chapters, and de la Pole is hard to discard, as he was an important man in the history of Holderness. It seems certain that William was from a merchant's family in Ravenser; he and his brother Richard were businessmen in Hull by the 1320s. He became very much the King's man, partly as a financier – of both Edward II and Edward III. It was from Edward II, who was struggling at the time, that he acquired Burstwick and Cleeton. Later, he faced wool smuggling charges, and at one time was imprisoned. His family were later to become the Dukes of Suffolk.

The other village in the proximity of Skipsea that was lost was Newhithe, or Hythe, referred to above. The scale of lost land in Skipsea itself through the latter half of the nineteenth century is on record – 1,593 acres in 1852, compared with 1,566 in 1891. George Poulson, in his comprehensive history of Holderness written in 1840, gives more details on the story of Hythe:

It is unnoticed in Domesday, but in the sheriff's return of all vills [a settlement that could be a parish, a manor or a tithing] 9E 11, it is joined with Skipsea and Cleeton. In 18E 11, when the parliament granted to the King a tenth or fifteenth, the Abbey of Meaux having suffered greatly from the devastating effects of the encroachment of the sea, represented their case to the King in Parliament for a reduction in assessments. ... There was in consequence an inquisition at Hull.

[Note: 9E 11 refers to the eleventh act of the ninth year of the reign of Elizabeth I – making the reference 1565.]

It was at that meeting that Meaux was granted the fish tithe, but then, as the record shows, 'The Meaux abbot bemoans that in 1396 the Hythe land has been totally destroyed.'

There is a telling little footnote in Cleeton history, though. In 1768, in a copyhold rental listing, we know the names and rentals paid of twenty-one tenants on the land later swept away. These included two women, and men with some wonderful names, such as Fontayn Osbaldiston and Cornwall Baron. The former paid £6 12s, and the latter 12s.

Even less is known of the other hamlet to be engulfed, Withow, but it is recorded that in the cliffs there the horns of an elk were found, together with trees, sticks, leaves and nuts.

The focus now shifts to Withernsea and the environs, which on Sheppard's map contains the lost villages of Monkwike, Owthorne and Newsham. Sheppard gives a full account of the loss of land around Withernsea; he makes a significant point about the use of groynes in the fight against the sea. Wooden groynes have been in use since the 1720s, and they are effective, but they have their limitations. At Mappleton, further up the Yorkshire coast, for instance, rock groynes were installed in 1991 and this stopped the loss of materials being moved along in that location. However, this had the effect of increasing erosion further south.

Owthorne, in 1823, had a listing in *Baines' Directory* of six farmers, two wheelwrights and six others, including a schoolmaster. Around that time, Owthorne had Waxholme, South Frodingham and Rimswell in its parish, and the total population in about 1830 was 415. In spite of losses to the sea, sixty years later, in *Bulmer's Directory* for 1892, there were thirteen farmers in Owthorne itself and also wheelwrights, carpenters and cow keepers in Rimswell.

In the popular journal *Old Yorkshire* for 1881, there is an account of Withernsea, and the groynes are given a special mention:

A stroll on the seashore, when the waves are rolling mighty billows onto the sands and washing away the clay cliffs, demonstrates forcibly the irresistible power of the ocean. Stand on the pier at Withernsea, when the wind is strong from the east, and the sight is grand. The water rolls up in great hills and valleys with a majestic sweep, curls in crescents of foam, dashing the spray high up in the air … and roars with a sullen sound, as if angry that its advances are repelled by the 'groins' [*sic*] that withstand its devastations. The 'groins' are formed of piles driven deep into the sand and clay, strong planks connecting the piles. The 'groins' are carried out in a straight line towards the low-water mark. They are placed about 100 yards apart and are effectual not only in helping to uphold the base of the clay cliffs, but gather an accumulation of the shifting sands.

Groynes at that time were not always the solution: the British weather saw to that. In 1867, in Whitstable, as one press report commented, 'Great injury was done to the shores by the washing away of the groins [*sic*] and beach.'

A major factor in the working of erosion on the Yorkshire coast is the phenomenon of longshore drift. This refers to the process of moving materials on a beach due to the angular movement of the waves coming onto the beach. The gradient of a beach affects that regular oblique wave movement and a severe storm can affect the whole process. Usually, the normal rate of erosion happens when the movement of beach material is caused by the waves coming at an angle. Their force forwards, called the swash, is followed by the recession – the backwash. This makes a shingle beach last only so long; the backwash and longshore drift takes it along, following the course of the oblique tide. This is how the lost pebbles and mud from the Yorkshire cliffs gradually shift along to Spurn to form a main shingle belt.

Sheppard carefully gives an account of Withernsea's land loss over the nineteenth century and earlier, but he starts with the groynes:

Opposite the village or town of Withernsea, the groynes, since their erection in 1870, have been helpful in preserving the sea front, and the promenade in more recent years has also assisted, as doubtless will the extension thereto just completed.

He noted the greater loss of land south of Withernsea itself, and that is exactly what happened in the Mappleton example:

Just south of Withernsea, there is a sudden and great increase in the breadth of the strip of land lost since 1852 and the Geological Surveyors found the coast had so altered in this part of Holderness that they had the 'new coast of 1881' engraved for their map instead of following the usual custom of putting their work on the old Ordnance Survey sheets.

The topic of groynes and their usefulness continued to attract discussion and debate well into the twentieth century. But even in the Edwardian years, most commentators saw the advantages of groynes, as in this feature from the *Sheffield Daily Telegraph* in 1904:

> The earlier heavy timber groynes, consisting of timber frames filled with chalk, proved fairly effective in breaking the force of the waves, but were too high to have proper effect in causing accretion on the foreshore. The later construction of four long, low timber groynes, however, had the result of causing, within three years, the accumulation of 500,000 tons of sand on the foreshore, raising the beach to an average height of about 4 feet over an area of 25,000 square yards.

Over the century since that feature, the same kind of groynes have been retained, but often backed by netted rock revetments, as has been done at Humberston, for instance. There, on the coast looking directly across to Spurn Head, the incoming tides are swift and ruthless, and even with modern technology and meteorology, there has to be constant vigilance on the low cliffs above the beaches.

The Royal Commission of 1911 was in no doubt as to what had been the problem at Withernsea:

> The Council have taken no measures but private enterprise about thirty years ago constructed groynes. Had the then owners effected repairs, it is possible the erosion would have been much reduced. ... The Council was not formed until 1898, and prior to that, no authority existed which was willing or able to do repairs.

Sheppard picks out examples of places lost. A typical instance is Neville's farm:

In 1763, Neville's farm contained 140 acres; and one 'close', adjoining the sea, was 10 chains [660 feet] long. In 1845, it was 6 chains long [390 feet], a loss of 144 yards in eighty-two years, or 1 yard, 2 feet a year. In 1911, the measurement had reduced from 7 chains to barely 3 chains, so that between 1845 and 1911, a further strip, 98 yards wide, has been washed away.

His images of Withernsea are very powerful. One shows the pier with the caption, 'This view shows the old pier, which, with the road in front of the picture, has been washed away by the sea.'

The pier was constructed in 1877, of iron. The 1891 directory explains what happened to it:

During a storm on 28 October 1880, a ship dashed through it, carrying away about 80 yards. The gap afterwards was repaired and connected with wooden piles; but the part extending beyond it was blown completely over by the fury of a storm on 25 March 1882. The pier was again seriously damaged just ten years after the first accident.

One thing we do know that was washed away to sea was the churchyard at Withernsea, in the fifteenth century. Sheppard notes that after an enquiry in 1444, it was decided that a new church should be built on Priest Hill. But he then adds, 'In 1488, the church was completed and consecrated. In the time of Henry VIII, the church was "much decayed" and in 1609, was damaged by a storm and was practically a ruin until a half-century ago.'

Close to Withernsea was Owthorne, written as 'Torne' in Domesday. This really is one of the clearest examples from the nineteenth century of a settlement annihilated by the sea. Sheppard points out that between 1852 and 1912, 'the road leading to Waxholme and Owthorne has been washed away. When this first happened, travellers had to go through a farmyard, but not long before Sheppard was writing, as he notes, 'a path made along the cliff edge for foot passengers, outside the farmyard has gone. As well as part of the farm buildings.' The most significant loss was Owthorne church, which went underwater in 1814, and by 1833, it was 18 yards from the cliff, out in the water.

John Phillips, writing in 1875, reported seeing, in 1826 at Owthorne, two gravestones, one with an inscription saying, 'I must lie here till Christ appear'. Soon after that, on another visit, he reported seeing 'bones of former generations washed out of the cliffs'. The sea reached as far as the churchyard by 1786, and soon after, work of reclamation and salvage began, with the chancel being taken down, and the parish registers were moved to Rimswell church, and as Sheppard commented, one recorded charge in the annals is for 'burying bones from the sand'.

A reference work of 1892 adds more information about this slippage into the sea:

> The sea here ... is continually encroaching on the land, and places and homesteads mentioned in old deeds now lie underwater. The church, which was known as the 'sister kirk', disappeared ... a large portion of the eastern end fell ... and coffins and bodies in various states of preservation were strewn upon the shore.

The following century brought more destruction. Nothing at all remained of the church by 1838, and in 1844, as the same work noted, 'the old parsonage house and two cottages shared the same fate.' In fact, 'Sister Kirk', or 'Sister Church', will be described again in chapter 8.

Poulson, in his monumental survey of Holderness published in the early nineteenth century, refers to what was saved from the churchyard: 'These relics of a departed greatness found a new place of sepulchre in Rimswell. In 1822, the chancel, nave and part of the tower were gone.'

As with the elk horn found at Hythe, there were strange finds at Owthorne, most notably a canoe. These items reached back to a very long time before civilized settlement, and gave hints of the natural history and early human habitation of the land before it was defined as coast. Thomas Sheppard describes one of the most significant:

> The shore, being for many years previously a fine sand, which was totally removed by the action of these violent tides, and a blue clay appeared upon which were prints of birds' feet, particularly swans, which are supposed to have been imprinted on the clay centuries ago. An old man remembered a canoe being found about sixty years before.

In the long catalogue of Sheppard's list of lost villages, one stands out as being very little known: Newsham. Sheppard adds the comment, however, that in Domesday it was said to comprise 600 acres. There was a chapel, and Drogo had in the area 'one sokeman, nine villeins and seven bordars'. The sokeman was a free tenant; villeins were unfree tenants who nevertheless had a certain share of the produce, and a bordar was at the lowest level, doing menial work, sometimes for a fixed payment.

Waxholme was in a similar position as far as Sheppard was concerned, and his book has an image showing 'all that is left of Waxholme'. The picture shows what appear to be two dwelling houses, a barn, a fence and one street lamp. Again, in previous centuries, a chapel had been recorded as being there, and in the early nineteenth century, some monitoring of the erosion took place because a 'preventive watch-house' was built at Sand-le-Mere. In 1833, it was just 84 yards from the coast. For Poulson, the place was 'devoid of all attraction'.

Other places that had entirely disappeared by Sheppard's time are Monkwike, which again was of some importance in the Domesday survey, though we know merely occasional landowners such as George Gower, who had lands there in 'soccage', which meant he held the land without a duty of military service. The same applies to Hilston, but the fight was on in Sheppard's time to preserve what could be worked on, such as Hilston church, which was rebuilt towards the end of the century.

In 1912, Thomas Sheppard provided the only real basis for any knowledge of these little communities. The hamlets and family farms were unluckily not placed in places that, in the terms used by modern geologists studying coastal erosion, are 'not defended', and so even as long ago as about 1900, the same priorities applied on the Yorkshire coast: that is, those with wealth and influence decided who and what would be preserved. But of course, even the new sea walls would not last forever. By the end of that busy and progressive nineteenth century, the holiday towns had been financed and developed; the stress had been placed on massive sea walls and promenades, but otherwise, in between Bridlington and Scarborough, the bays and cliffs were left alone to disappear at a slow rate, while the line of coastal communities south of Bridlington placed outside Hornsea and Withernsea were left to cope on their own.

The focus now shifts to a survival: the Spurn headland. The notion of loss and gain now arises, and the narrative begins to include such things as railways and lighthouses.

Chapter 5

The Grandeur of Kilnsea and Spurn

On one side lay the ocean and on one
Lay a great water, and the moon was full.
Alfred Lord Tennyson, *Idylls of the King*

I f there was one event in the chronicles of the history of this staggeringly awesome headland, it would be this brief notice from the *Morning Chronicle* in 1814:

By a letter from Spurn Light House we have the following melancholy account: that on Friday morning last … at seven o'clock, a large three-mast ship struck on the New Sand near that place; at eleven o'clock, the people on board got up the main and mizzen top-masts; at twelve, the masts went overboard and all hands, sixteen or eighteen in number, perished without a possibility of rendering them assistance, the sea being so tempestuous … and although great exertions have been made to find out to what place this unfortunate vessel belonged, they have hitherto proved ineffectual.

Things to note here: first of all, although there was a lifeboat, it never had a chance to approach anywhere near the vessel; also, the ship was so ravaged that there was no information about her; and lastly, it all happened in the hurly-burly of a tempest. Those elements define the majestic but lethal terrain of Spurn.

Spurn seen from the air looks fragile. From up above, one may see that it is a long neck, with a very slim rod between the more substantial parts. But that view adds to the certainty that it would take no more than one of the sea's rages to lash away the fragile shingle and banks, clinging onto their identity against the odds. As you walk into it, from Kilnsea, there is a false sense of security because to the right are fields and to the left there are bushes and thick grass: it could be any English meadow. But when the walker reaches the narrow part of the spit, mud and pebbles all around suggest something as vulnerable as a sandcastle.

The villages that have been listed and described in previous chapters were, or partly still are, placed along a sweep of curving coastline extending for more than 40 miles, and their cliffs are not particularly high, being of brown clay, and forming a distinctly different impression on visitors when compared to the chalk cliffs further up the coast past Flamborough. After the brief accounts of the lost places off that coast, the focus now shifts to Kilnsea and Spurn, and their especially grand, awesome nature, which has been retained today, after the vicissitudes of their historical experience.

Kilnsea sits at the base of what becomes Spurn Head, reaching out into the North Sea and curving around into the Humber mouth, and on its northern side it is close to the lost villages of Out Newton and Dimlington, along with Old Kilnsea, all listed by Thomas Sheppard in 1912 on his comprehensive map. The traveller, after seeing Kilnsea, may walk out onto Spurn, and there will be the great North Sea to his left and the Humber clays to his right, which form great extents of mud. It is a sobering thought to reflect that the sea bed around here is littered with fragments of what once were those places that have already been listed as eaten up by the waves.

At Dimlington, the Easington gas terminal dominates the landscape. It has been there since 1967, and one might think that the sight of it would deter investigators more interested in the sea bed than in pipelines. But in 2009, the Seasearch group North East did a dive; marine biology was the area of research in question. They helped to find information on what might have remained there of any past constructions done by humans; but the focus was on starfish and crabs.

Medieval Dimlington was largely in the hands of the Abbot of Meaux, and court rolls from 1313 show that this land was so fertile that the Abbot received 'eight pounds sterling for a fine', but of course, the land was going even then, and one record has this comment: 'Of the above, 20 oxgangs which were daily wasting by the action of the sea, were lost; 55 acres were entirely lost and they were worth 2s 6d an acre.'

Cobles at Filey, with the Brig behind.

The lodgings where Charlotte Brontë stayed in Filey.

Cobles at Filey, by the Yacht Club.

This is where the road ends at Skipsea.

A warning sign with obvious dangers.

The Coastguard building by the Filey prom.

The threat of the waves is seen dramatically here in Filey at high tide.

A long view of Filey prom.

The disintegration of the cliffs at Filey is obvious.

This is a close view of the soft cliff material at Filey.

A section of cliff already down at Filey.

Groynes at Hornsea being strengthened.

A closer view of the Hornsea groynes.

The fury of the
waves is vivid here.

This image shows the desperate measures taken at Hornsea a century ago. (Sheppard: *The Lost Towns of the Yorkshire Coast*)

A picture of Hornsea a century ago. (Sheppard: *The Lost Towns of the Yorkshire Coast*)

Part of what was once a home.

The foundation of a building once at Spurn.

A beautiful stretch of Spurn beach.

ROUGH SEA - NORTH BAY. SCARBOROUGH.

A rough sea hitting the Scarborough coast.

The club at Skipsea – 100 yards from the cliff edge.

These homes by the sea at Skipsea have tiny residual lawns.

A view of the piles of debris on the Spurn beach.

A bundle of masonry – once a home at Spurn.

A solid piece of building at Spurn.

A panoramic view of the estuary and lighthouse at Spurn.

What the sea can do to a manmade road.

The lifeboat at Withernsea.

The castle-like remnant of former sea front, Withernsea.

The distinctive Withernsea lighthouse.

A common image now: great rock lines facing the waves.

John Smeaton's map, showing some places now gone. (Sheppard: *The Lost Towns of the Yorkshire Coast*)

This milestone, now gone, shows once useful information. (Sheppard: *The Lost Towns of the Yorkshire Coast*)

In 1911, when Thomas Sheppard wrote his book, this was all that remained of Auburn. (Sheppard: *The Lost Towns of the Yorkshire Coast*)

An old print of the Marine Hotel, Hornsea. (Sheppard: *The Lost Towns of the Yorkshire Coast*)

In 1800, Owthorne church was still clinging on. (Sheppard: *The Lost Towns of the Yorkshire Coast*)

This map shows the former line of the coast at Kilnsea. (Sheppard: *The Lost Towns of the Yorkshire Coast*)

This plaque gives some startling information – placed in a wall at Kilnsea. (Sheppard: *The Lost Towns of the Yorkshire Coast*)

A picture of one of the climmers egg collectors at Bempton. (Sheppard: *The Lost Towns of the Yorkshire Coast*)

Note: All pictures by the author, unless otherwise stated.

Kilnsea and neighbouring settlements were closely inspected in the Royal Commission of 1911, and the writers of the following report were aware of the urgency required concerning the loss of land:

The maintenance of the Spurn is of the utmost importance to the preservation of the mouth of Humber, as a harbour of refuge, into which ships of all nations, navigating the North Sea, of whatever draft, may run at all states of the tide, there being no bar at the mouth of the river.

Only three years later, when the Great War began, this urgency was plain for all to see, and gun positions, a railway, and housing for workers and their families were soon to be established. But Kilnsea itself, together with the neighbouring villages of Skeffling, Easington and Patrington, have a rich and informative history with regard to their relationship with the sea. Writing in 1835, George Head traversed that route, from east of Hull right out to Spurn, and on the way, he takes time to report on the nature of the Kilnsea to Spurn roads, but he also adds a rare glimpse into the sort of community that was always under threat of flood:

These corn factors possess large magazines at the small port of Patrington Haven, a mile distant from Patrington, at the mouth of a creek which communicates with the Humber, so that we have a direct communication with the vast depositaries of grain at Wakefield. ... The village consists of only a few houses, in number apparently inadequate to the size of the magazines.

Kilnsea, described in 1891 in the directory, is related to the 'Chilnesse' of Domesday. The manor there was given to Drogo, whom we met at Skipsea. The directory immediately locates the threat of the sea as the distinctive element of the village's identity, and describes the loss of the old church of St Helen, noting that in 1823, it was no longer a safe place to hold a service. Then we have:

It was dismantled in 1826, and in August that year the nave and chancel together with the tower, were swallowed up by the sea. ... The spot where it stood is now under the sea and can be seen only at very low ebb tides.

In 1891, Kilnsea had six people working farmland, two inns (the Blue Bell and the Crown and Anchor), but the emphasis was on official work against the waves. The directory lists C. Hopper as master of the Spurn signal station, John Ombler, superintendent of the Spurn beach and works, and Thomas Winson, master of the lifeboat.

Fortunately, oral history has provided rare accounts of life in Kilnsea and Spurn in the late Victorian and Edwardian years. Ernest Medforth Norwood, for instance, wrote in his memoirs the story of the loss of the church:

When the church collapsed in 1826, some of the gravestones were moved to Easington and can be seen in the north of the churchyard. When the church was in a dangerous state, services were held in one of my great-grandfather's houses [he was responsible for the Crown and Anchor being built]. His grave is in St Helen's churchyard and he was a cousin of Lord Tennyson.

This was surely Medforth Tennison, who died in 1893.

Ernest also left an account of what it was like over a century ago to live by the side of such a threat:

Villagers found much washed up on the sea or the Humber shore. It was quite a usual thing to find a barrel of herring. ... Also, a lot of timber and pit props floated in. One Saturday I went down on the Humber side and gathered over 100 wooden blocks that were used for street-laying in Hull. ... Coal was washed up now and again. This was known as sea coal and made a good fire. ... Once a ship struck a mine, and bags of flour, boxes of butter, lard and margarine were washed up.

Sheppard, writing in 1912, is thorough in dealing with Kilsea, as he always is, and he comments that at that time, 'The Humber side of Kilnsea is suffering.' He then does the usual analysis of a specific place, in this case the Blue Bell inn:

The Blue Bell was built at Kilnsea in 1847, and according to the record inserted into the wall, was then 534 yards from the cliff. In 1852, it was 527 yards away; in 1876, it was 396 yards away; in 1888, 377 yards. In 1898, Canon Maddock measured and found it to be 328 yards away and Mr Backhouse (1908) measured it as 200 yards.

Sheppard would have been glad to know the situation today. The Kilnsea folk, after an enclosure award in the 1840s, rebuilt their homes. Their lives were about fishing and farming. As the Kilnsea Reborn website states:

> Before the loss of the village, Kilnsea had several ale houses, shops and even a school. After the new village was created, it never got larger than about thirty houses, though it did manage to retain two public houses, the Blue Bell and the Crown and Anchor.

Items were re-gathered, such as the medieval font that had been stored at Skeffling; church registers were brought back; and there was some new building. Today, in spite of a heavy storm in 2013 that caused a severe flood, there is a new Kilnsea. There is a determination that the village will not go the way of Old Kilnsea, which as late as the eighteenth century still had part of the land described in Domesday, although the east field had been lost.

The success in the battle with the sea then, stems from the 1840 Enclosure Act, which allowed the local people to rebuild, and they sensibly shifted locations towards the Humber. To go there today is a very pleasant experience. There is a neat car park close to the caravans and cliffs, and the walk into Spurn is on a good road bordered by very thriving farmland to the right, and there is a general awareness that the bird life is being preserved as well as closely observed.

In 1912, Sheppard offers a catalogue of distances and coastal recession. However, he wisely supplies a map to show the overall loss across the whole length of Old Kilnsea. The 'east field' mentioned above is included in that map, and Sheppard has this material also, quoting a writer called Thompson in 1824:

There is no doubt that Kilnsea was formerly of considerable height above the town. A clergyman who had lived to old age in that part of Holderness, and died not many years ago, was often heard to assert that he remembered a field, called the east field, lying between Kilnsea and the sea, which greatly rose in height towards the sea, but no east field can now [1824] be found and there is no doubts that it was all swept away by the sea before the end of the last century.

There had been a serious flood shortly before, in 1905–06, and Sheppard wrote in his study that the low lands from Kilnsea Warren nearly to Easington Lane end on the north and beyond Skeffling on the west, were flooded, breaking through some artificial banks. He shows very powerful images from those events, including a panorama of Kilnsea, totally flooded, and the road at Easington, nearby, completely underwater.

Spurn itself is staggeringly beautiful. It has the magnificence we always associate with wildness, with something elementally untouched, and this is in spite of the fact that the 3 miles of thin sand, marram grass, shingle and modern human settlement in vestigial form have cluttered some parts of it.

I arrived there on my first visit in early spring, and parked by a crumbling cliff at Kilnsea, bordered by caravans and a small pool where deer were drinking. It was a time before visitors arrived in any numbers, and I saw later that the only other people there were bird watchers, with their cameras and tripods set up above the seaside beach. To the other side there was just mud. As I walked towards the first part of Spurn, where there are some buildings and foundations of former buildings, the atmosphere was one of industry and business on the farm side, and on the nature reserve the birdsong was loud and pleasing.

Reaching the second stretch of the headland, which is sand and stones, bordered by mudflats on the Humber side, there was a slight sense of menace. Walking there, I felt a certain vulnerability, even though the lighthouse was seen in the distance, beyond a bank of vegetation. But it was on the beach that the voices of history could be heard, speaking through the fragments and mixtures of stone on the ground. The beach there is strewn with chunks of rock, and great slabs of brickwork that were once part of a house.

Back in 1835, George Head did the same journey, and he sensed the same threat: 'The approach to the lighthouse is across a sand bank, covered with hard turf, barely covered with herbage, and perforated with rabbit burrows in every direction. The whole of this sand bank, that is to say, every part exposed to the sea, appears to be receiving augmentation, rather than sustaining diminution, for it is situated upon a point of confluence of currents, where the contributions of the soil are greater, on the average, than the quantity carried away. Generally ... the ravages of the waves on the coast are considerable. ... At all events, the site of the lighthouse, for the present, seems quite secure; though, as a place of habitation, in dreary winter weather, at the end of a narrow spit of land, and menaced on three sides by the tumultuous ocean, the prospect may be dreary and awful.

Head located the palpable sense of menace and openness to nature; he said little about the great expanse of clay on the Humber side. There, from the tip of Spurn all the way around to the Easington Clays by Long Bank Bridge, and then even further down towards Paull, the deposition of muddy sediments continues. The names on the maps say it all: Old Den and Greedy Gut. Someone thought of those names with a touch of burning resentment inside that Nature had won some skirmishes in this long war.

Of course, the crucially important item on Spurn is the lighthouse, and the history of this lighthouse is long and detailed. This story has been told with exemplary scholarship by G. De Boer in a monograph for the East Yorkshire Local History Society, and every minute detail in the making of the succession of buildings is there. But essentially, in the modern period, the story begins with Justin Angell's building of 1673–74, and then a century later, John Smeaton's 1766 work on the project, completed in 1772, when he had made two towers. When Trinity House was involved later, there were two structures, and they were known as low light versions, being swept away by the mid-nineteenth century. These had been lit by the burning of stone coal, something of inferior composition, similar to shale, which burned slowly. Smeaton's lighthouse lasted until the 1890s, until a new one was made.

Smeaton, born in Austhorpe, near Leeds in 1724, showed his engineering genius in a number of ways, but in terms of the present context, after he visited Holland in 1754 he learned a lot about land, sea and human settlements. As a Victorian writer, R.V. Taylor, summed up, 'He obtained an acquaintance with the construction of embankments, artificial navigations and similar works and these formed an important part of his engineering education.' After he made his famous Eddystone Lighthouse, he wrote on that project and added an appendix on the building of the Spurn light. Therefore, we know quite a lot about what he did there. By the time he left the place for the last time in 1786, he had made the 'swape' – a light on a thin pole supported by struts – and a 'low light', which was 50 feet high. The latter was finished in 1776.

The force behind the later Spurn lights was Trinity House, a guild described later on, but it is worth mentioning here that this self-help group, formed in 1369 by Robert Marshall, had a literary celebrity describe them: this was Stephen Taylor, known as 'The Water Poet', who visited Hull in 1662 and published *A Very Merry Wherry-Ferry Voyage or Yorke for my Money*, in which we have this explanation of the Trinity House society:

> Besides for every sea or marine cause, they have a house of Trinity, whose laws and orders do confirm, or else reform that which is right, or that which wrongs deform; it is a comely built, well ordered place, but that which most of all the house doth grace are rooms for widows, who are old and poor, and have been wives to mariners before. They are for house room, food, or lodging or for firing, Christianly provided for, and as some die, some doth their places win, as one goes out, another doth come in.

Of more interest than the light itself, for the purpose of this narrative, is the community living there over the years as various lights were made. In the medieval period, the spit, after the ruin of Ravenserodd, became known as Ravens Spurn or Ravenspur. Shakespeare refers to that place, calling it Ravenspurgh, because it was significant as the place where the future Henry IV landed when he returned to claim his crown from Richard II, who had earlier banished him. As early as 1427, there had been a petition for permission to make a lighthouse at the spit, and the material relating to this and following attempts to create a light give us information on what Spurn was like. In 1567, for instance, as the main historian of the lighthouses notes, we have this:

> Ravensey Spurn is a sandy hill environed and compassed about upon the sea side with the sea and with the Humber, containing 6 acres whereupon is neither arable land, meadow not pasture … neither anything else but a few short scrubby thorns.

After this, there were a number of lights installed, from Justinian Angell's of 1674 to the one built in 1895. Of most interest for present purposes is the habitation there. Pictures from the late nineteenth century show the lighthouse with a strong, high surrounding wall; another shows a row of houses with firm emplacements along their frontage, with Smeaton's lighthouse 100 yards in front, in the water. In the foreground a woman stands, swaddled in clothes, on a deserted beach.

There was at that time a constant threat to the life on Kilnsea and Spurn, and one of the most intense and violent assaults from the sea was in the floods of 1906, captured on film by Hull photographer Mr Blenkin. His picture shows a small group of people on a neck of land, being thrashed by high waves and a strong wind. In the novel *The Doctor's Lass*, written by local writer Edward Booth and published in 1910, we have an account of that time in a passage in which a doctor has to travel to a patient:

> For all that lay in front of him distinguishable from this living volume of water, the Doctor might have been setting his mare's nose to the North Sea. In no place along the roadway would there lie a greater depth of water than 4 feet; but this was water in motion, driven by the sea and whipped up by the wind.

Over the last two centuries, the inhabitants on Spurn have ranged from Coastguard staff to military men, and railway workers to lighthouse keepers. Families have had to live there too. The story of the Coastguard illustrates the tough life there. The station was established in 1810, and the end of their presence there came in 2016. Six families moved out in that year. The media reported the end of the service there and one article quoted a spokesman from the RNLI, who said:

Our crew make many sacrifices to enable them to save lives at sea – a role they would be unable to carry out without the full support of their families – and the RNLI has a duty of care to both its crew members and their families.

Those families were there over the years, behind the men in the old photographs, such as the 1900 crew of ten men in solid garb, which looks like an outfit of two massive ammunition belts or perhaps the Pirelli tyre man. Other pictures from the archive show ten men and a dog, so clearly there was a fairly large community there over the nineteenth and twentieth centuries. If we want an immediate image that shows the rawness of life out there, then it is a photograph showing the line of terraced houses open to the elements, with their small patch of sand around them, or the lighthouse with its circular wall suggesting more a castle than a few homes.

The crew also had men based at Easington, close by. In 1883, for instance, they were called into action when two brigs from Scarborough ran aground near Kilnsea, and the press reported that the crew turned out 'with their rocket apparatus' and they rescued all the men but one. This technology was the Dennett Rocket, invented in 1827 by John Dennett and installed gradually at Coastguard stations; by 1853, 120 stations had them. Their value was shown as early as 1832, when their use saved nineteen sailors' lives. These were shore to ship rockets that would supply a lifeline.

Victorian narrative painting loved shipwrecks and images of noble seamen at work against the torrents and gales. The rocket gave an added element to that, but many pictures, such as *Launching the Lifeboat*, by Thomas Brookes (who was born in Hull in 1818) show the harsh reality of a lifeboat in action. His picture depicts the whole family behind the men pushing the stern of the boat, and all around them the storm rages with such intensity that the sea and the rain are indistinguishable. Brookes knew the coast here and he wanted to show the world what the lifeboat community was like and how it had to live. Later he painted *Saved*, which showed the return of the boat, and he took these lines from a poem by Elizabeth Barratt Browning to go with the picture:

All the helpless are safe, the brave boat nears the shore,
The true hearts who saved them are with us once more.

The full history of the Spurn lifeguard community has been written by Barry Herbert in *Lifeboats of the Humber*, and he describes there the beginnings of the little community. The concept came when the Trinity House Brethren liked the design and proposal for a boat by a boat builder called Henry Greathead, from South Shields. A Mr Iveson told Trinity House that the owner, Mr Constable, would build a boathouse and provide the crew. Barry Herbert gives a fascinating account of what the master of the boat and his people would do:

> The means of livelihood for the Master was to be the managing of the tavern, which was to be part of the facilities at Spurn Point. He would sell poultry, vegetables, and provisions to vessels (numbering approx 500 a year that came to Spurn to ballast with cobbles and gravel). The Master would also cater for the labourers and any visitors who came from time to time. Mr Iveson said that the twelve able-bodied men who were to man the lifeboat would come from Kilnsea.

The cottages built on Spurn were financed by Trinity House; they were sorely needed, as the lifeboat crew had at first used a disused barracks. Trinity House called for a public subscription for the funds; the end house of the first cottages was the *Lifeboat Inn*. But a row of houses was built to replace them in 1858. The crew had to wait for a proper lifeboat house though: that was not installed until 1913, when the RNLI were running the show.

The family life on Spurn was really hard, and their resolve was often severely tested, as in 1904, when the *Hull Daily Mail* gave this snippet of news:

> Owing to the deficiency of drinking water at Spurn Head the families are now reduced to an allowance of six bucketfuls per week per family. The *Lifeboat Inn* depends for its water supply entirely on the rainwater tank at the lighthouse.

Of course, there were several families there, and so there were children who needed an education. In October 1890, a school building was built by a Hull firm, Lison's. It cost £170 and the dimensions were 26 feet by 20 feet, with six windows and a coke stove in the centre of the floor. Teaching began in early 1891, with twenty children attending; a few years later, the school was opened up to all children in the broader area around Spurn, rather than catering simply for the lifeboat families.

In the first years of the twentieth century, everything changed in terms of the running of the lifeboat here; the Hull Conservancy Board took over, at the time when there were nationwide moves to create such outfits (the Thames had one, for instance). There was a long period of wrangling and bad feeling between that organization and the RNLI. By 1911, the latter organization took over.

Writing in 2010, Chris Horan, dealing with Humber shipping and social history, used extensive interviews and oral history for his material, and he referred to a memoir by George Jarratt, who had knowledge of the lifeboat at Spurn in the 1880s. George had some valuable insights to give, and Chris Horan summarized:

> The isolation of the community is brought home by one quote: 'We children did not know the worth of money, there being no shops nearer than 8 miles away. We could get a few boiled sweets when one of the boats sailed across to Grimsby, taking their crabs to market there. They used to take a sailor bag and a list from each housewife, of groceries they needed and brought them back.'

Some of George's memories are startling to today's readers, perhaps seeming medieval: 'The lifeboat folk ate wild rabbits, blackbird, starlings and rooks and the occasional wild duck. There were also the fruits of the sea and the occasional bag of ship's biscuits.' Other aspects of life have echoes of the kinds of activities necessitated by the Second World War:

> The families had to plan ahead and fend for themselves. The main meat was rolled sides of bacon. They also had home-grown potatoes reared in sand and seaweed, Hornsea herring, apples and flour. Some members of the community kept a few hens and a pig.

It was certainly isolated. Chris Horan reported George's point about this:

The only land-bound people they saw regularly were the postman and a preacher from Patrington Primitive Methodist Circuit, who would ride by trap to Kilnsea and walk the rest of the way before conducting a service in an upper room of the lighthouse. Sunday school general schooling was in the Coxwain's house, with the same room being the telegraph station and the post office.

From that time to today, a trip to see the lighthouse is definitely a must for visitors to Holderness. Back in the 1930s, when Ella Pontefract and Marie Hartley made a tour of Yorkshire, they went to Spurn. Their account captures perfectly the draw of that wildness, and the sheer loneliness of the headland:

There is no road beyond Kilnsea. You must walk over the soft, sinking sand to it or get a permit to travel in the army trolley. We rode out with the postman and a party of girl guides from Hull, who munched sweets and sang a lively song with a refrain beginning:

> For we're all down in t'cellar 'oile,
> Where t'mud slarts on t'winders

They seemed unmoved by this strange scene as they would have been by a Hull street.

What has been lost from Spurn is best understood from old photographs. The main danger over the last century and more is the fragmentation of the spit into a series of islands. At one point, groynes and embankments were emplaced, in order to try to preserve the solid spine of land down the centre of the headland, and so in the end it is spending money that will succeed in preservation here.

What has to be recalled in trying to understand this area and the story of these lost communities is the basic nature of Holderness, and this needs a look before the focus shifts to the most significant of all the lost towns – Ravenser. Holderness, as has often been said, is very different from the rest of Yorkshire. Before the Local Government Act of 1888, the name related to a very old administrative tract, with the designation 'wapentake'. This was the name used in the Northern counties for a *hundred*: this is a division of a shire, probably dating from the 1000s; some historians think that the name stemmed from a unit of 100 families, but that is disputed. My story so far has been of this coast being worn away by what is often called the 'north-easterly fetch', and in contrast to the action of nature to soak the land of Holderness, the river Hull drains it. The Hull and its coastal streams have caused the terrain of Holderness to be one with flood banks, and of course, there will be tidal surges, which have been the reason for the establishment of the River Hull Tidal Surge Barrier. The basic reason for the problems of drainage and flooding over the centuries stem from the flatness of the land, which will not drain naturally. At the heart of all the drainage is the Holderness Drain, which was first worked on in 1764 by John Grundy.

In the early twentieth century – a time in which so much of the subjects of the current story exist (as in Sheppard's accounts) – Holderness was integrated very strongly in Winifred Holtby's modern classic, *South Riding*, in which she has the 'Cold Harbour Colony'. Her description of their home is intensely informative about the poorer communities at the time:

Cold Harbour Colony owed its existence to a nineteenth-century philanthropist, Sir Rupert Colderdyke, who believed in making 2 acres grow where one had been before. He had set thorn fences in mud of the Leame Estuary, against which receding tides piled clay and driftwood that slowly from week to week grew from piles to banks, from banks to shallow islands, from islands to outworks of the coast itself, then mile by mile, into level, arable land, lightish towards the river where the tides drained off the clay and heavy as pudding farther in.

Again, before moving on to consider the medieval period, a few background facts will help. As has been noted in earlier chapters, Drogo, given land by William the Conqueror, was an earlier ruler, and then the land was later passed to Stephen of Aumale, in 1102. What became known as the Honour of Holderness was passed down through the Aumale earldom, through to William de Forz, who died in 1260. The Crown took over ownership by *escheat* – an obstruction in a line of descent, which meant that the land had to revert to the original owner – in this case, the King of England.

At the high point of the Middle Ages, Holderness, with its coastline and its many streams and tides, was an area deemed to be distant from centres of power. The church owned a lot of land also, and abbeys had considerable land ownership. Over all this – lords and abbots – there was the Crown. There was plenty to work for, though: as Isaac Leatham wrote in 1794:

> The East Riding, which is the least of the three divisions [*ridings* of Yorkshire] has a dry, sandy and barren soil in general, but towards the sea coast the valleys are very fertile and the woods produce corn, and feed great numbers of black cattle.... The sea near the coast swarms with herrings, large turbots and a great variety of other fish.

With this in mind, it becomes understandable that such places as abbeys in York wanted land out in the more lonely parts of Yorkshire. The sea had some advantages, after all.

The lords of the manors wanted every penny they could squeeze from their tenants, as is shown in records of accounts where they survive. In an antiquarian magazine from 1880, a correspondent sent in to the editor a manuscript book that had been found, and it referred to Burstwick, in Holderness. The list was an account 'of all the men's names and the rent they pay unto Matthew Appleyard in the Preston Lordship for his lands there'. The list includes money from the wealthy, such as Francis Hylbert, who rented several 'oxgangs' of land – and that classification could range from a few acres up to as many as 50 acres, depending on the soil. The *oxgang* was originally supposed to be 'the amount of land that could support a knight and his family for a year', as defined by historian John Richardson. The list goes down to the poorest tenants, such as 'The Skrogge closses in Rich. Whit's use ... £4'. This refers to a group of small, low-value lands (*closes*), which were probably used for keeping a few pigs or hens. The overall list has sixty pieces of land or small property all earning cash for Matthew.

Those tenants would have been living daily lives entirely typical of people across Holderness: keeping animals, fishing, doing small trading and offering any service they could. That was the English rural life for centuries: even as recent as the 1950s, in many Yorkshire villages, there was still a reliance on barter, and people survived on very little productivity for a market. The need for subsistence was paramount. Fortunately for Holderness, there was an abundance of fish everywhere.

This is where the notion of trade (and smuggling, which appears in chapter 7) enter the narrative. That is the ideal moment to shift the attention to a town once remarkable and powerful, off Spurn, which now lies under the sea: Ravenser, also called Ravenser Odd.

Chapter 6

Ravenser Odd and Holderness

Little drops of water, little grains of sand
Make the mighty ocean and the pleasant land.

Julia Carney, *Little Things*

L ost communities are usually small, insignificant places that never figured in the broader advance of history; they are on the margins in every sense, and are outstandingly ordinary, with that anonymity Thomas Gray found in an English country churchyard. There may have been 'mute, inglorious Miltons' buried there, but no chronicle ever recorded their lives. However, on rare occasions, the disappeared cluster of homes and public buildings actually figures significantly in social or political history. Such a place was Ravenser, along with another tiny satellite, Odd. Writers muddled the names and called it Ravenser or Ravenserodd, or any number of other names. The Vikings were fond of naming places after ravens, with their prefix 'hrafne' defining a headland or an inlet.

Ravenser did become a significant place, though only for as long as it could stay above water.

Some lost locations are mythic; they may rival Atlantis in their accumulation of folklore and narrative. If Yorkshire has one, it was a little way off Spurn, and it was once a community that could not be ignored. It made friends and enemies, and it was mixed up in wars and the lives of kings.

In the *Strand Magazine* of October 1901, there was a feature headed 'The Lost Land of England', which featured an account of a place called 'Ravensere'. The piece contained a drawing of this town, and Thomas Sheppard was astonished at this, because no known image of the place existed as far as he knew. Sheppard wrote that he enquired of the publishers, Newnes, where the illustration was from. The publishers could not answer and asked the author, a Mr Beckles Wilson; he, too, could not give an answer.

The picture shows a prominent church tower in the centre, and two rows of houses, with trees behind. It would have warmed the hearts of Sheppard and everyone else interested in the lost towns if there had been a source for the picture. What the feature did show was that there is a mystique about lost communities, and that tends to generate myths and stories.

A recent visitor, Tom Blass, researching his book *The Naked Shore*, points out one of the place's key moments in history:

> Raveners – *Hrafn reyni* – was always nowheresville, even at the end of the first millennium, but it warranted a mention in the Icelandic sagas as the place where the Norse army of Harald Hardrada embarked on its voyage home following its defeat by Harold Godwinson at Stamford Bridge.

Blass also reminds the reader of some of the features of the early medieval place – noting that it had a harbour, customs house, prison, windmills and a church. These details come from the early pipe rolls, and they are described by later historians such as J.R. Boyle, as he translates many of the Latin originals.

Sheppard reproduces the picture in his own book and adds as his caption, 'Alleged view of Ravenspurne (probably a forgery).' The settlement itself has been given a number of names throughout history. It lay somewhere off Spurn, further out to sea, and not very far from Grimsby (which will be an important fact later in this chapter). Sheppard, in considering the origin of the place, wrote about a theory expressed by William Shelford in 1869:

> He points out that, even in Roman times, Spurn Point must have been 2,250 yards at least beyond the present coastline; and that at or near this spot the Danes landed in 867, planted their standard 'The Raven' and practically originated the town of Ravensberg or Ravenser, or Ravensere.

On his map, Sheppard locates Ravenspurn and Ravenser Odd, as the two places had been referred to by various writers, but it seems that they were really one place.

However, alternative thinking, based on written sources, argues that a town called Ravenser was created from a shingle bank, off Spurn, and that became a significant township, with two MPs, fairs, markets and other elements of civilization. Beresford, whose work on lost towns was referred to in the last chapter, agrees that it was one of two settlements that developed 'in the shifting sands of the Humber around Spurn Point', and adds that the locations of both settlements have been lost to the sea. The various names involving the 'raven' component have certainly caused confusion over the years.

A full account of Ravenser, or Ravenserodd, as seems to be a full nomenclature for what was there, was written by J.R. Boyle in 1889. His account is in no doubt that the community was made, starting out as an island, and he quotes and translates a range of original source documents in his history. He begins with a Hundred Roll of 1276, in which a town called Odd was named, and called at the same time Ravenserodd. In these rolls its origin is explained:

> Forty years ago by the casting up of the sea, sand and stones accumulated, on which accumulation William de Fortibus [also *Forz* spelling], then Earl of Albemarle, began to build a certain town which is called Ravenserodd and it is an island; the sea surrounds it.

These Hundred Rolls were produced from the shire courts that came into being in the tenth century; their existence is a boon to medieval historians, and without them, one wonders whether we know anything at all about such places as Ravenser.

William, who died in 1242, was from a French family originating in Poitou. In the reign of John, the Albemarle estates were established, and this land included the wapentake of Holderness. He had, as was explained in the previous chapter, the castle at Skipsea as well as some Lincolnshire property. He was caught up in the struggles between King John and the barons, which led to the Magna Carta and the following conflicts as Parliament emerged.

Thankfully, we have a chronicle written by Abbot Burton of the abbey at Meaux on the Humber, which will figure in the next chapter, and this gives a clear explanation of the place:

The former Ravensserre, where now nothing remains except a single manor house with its appurtenances, and which is in-land, and distant both from the sea and the Humber, is called Ald Ravenseere.... But that town of Ravenserodd ... occupying a position in the utmost limits of Holderness ... was distant from the mainland a space of 1 mile or more. For access to which from ancient times from Ald Ravensere a sandy road extended covered with round and yellow stones, thrown up in a little time by the height of the floods, having a breadth which an archer can scarcely shoot across, and wonderfully maintained by the tides of the sea on its east side and by the ebb and flow of the Humber on its west side. Which road yet remains visible ... but for the space of half a mile, has been washed into the Humber since those days.... Of the site of Ravensere Odd, scarcely a vestige remains.

This makes complete sense on the evidence of other sources and opinions. The two communities were once linked, but were made at first into two islands as the path was washed away; then Odd disappeared, leaving Ravenser. The latter became, as will now be seen, a place of real importance from the early thirteenth century through to about 1380. Sheppard comments that by 1390, all trace of the town was gone. The island off Spurn, then, had a period of successful trading and identity for about 160 years, going from about 1235, when William de Fortibus developed it, to 1390.

Ravenser was undoubtedly an important place, but it first attracts notice when in conflict with the town of Grimsby across the Humber mouth. We know what Ravenser had at the beginning of its period of life, because the Abbot of Meaux acquired land there, granted by William. The monks gained:

a place ... with appurtenances, containing half an acre of land in the borough ... and we may construct for ourselves buildings suitable for our store of herring and other kinds of fish ... and besides he confirmed to us the aforesaid rent of Ald Ravenser.

The latter place was, as we have seen, doomed. William was not giving very much.

In 1251, the King gave a charter to William de Fortibus, giving Ravenser a fair and a market, and in 1256, there is a significant statement: that Ravenser was a port. When this was done, the award also stated that there could be no other port between Ravenser and Scarborough. Its day had come. If it was by then a place of importance, what land did it have? The charter refers to 16 *bovates* of land. As with all these medieval terms relating to land, the area named is variable; a *bovate* was thought to be around an eighth of a *hide*, which makes it a flexible concept that probably averaged about 17–20 acres. Even if we allow a conservative figure of 10 acres per *bovate*, that makes Ravenser in 1256 a place of 160 acres.

Then the problems began. As Ravenser grew and had a valued status in the eyes of the Crown, there emerged economic rivalry. The issue was one concerning *forestalling*. The Grimsby men put on paper their grievance, explaining this offence:

The men of the said town of Ravensodd go out with their boats into the high sea where there are ships carrying merchandise, and intending to come to Grimsby. ... The said men hinder those ships and lead them to Ravenserodd by force when they cannot amicably persuade them to go hither.

The Grimsby men told officials that Ravenserodd was 'but a tide away' from them and it was stealing their trade. The Ravenser men were in favour, though. In 1286, they had been given by letters patent the right to sell bread and beer in the town. This makes it clear that the place had visitors, and indeed had 'punters'. They were entrepreneurs, making the most of limited resources. The orders from the Crown forbade strangers to arrive and sell bread and beer: it was basic economic protection for this new town on the scene.

But the pressure from Grimsby continued. In 1290, the King issued a writ of enquiry, so that Grimsby's complaint could be fully investigated. The king in question was Edward I and his enquiry promised to be thorough, telling his commissioners that they should go to Grimsby on a day appointed and 'make inquisition there' with the county sheriff present, and that 'all knights and upright loyal men' should have their say. The commissioners reported in full. It was a report that allowed a lot to Ravenser, and in the course of the questions and answers, there is a very vivid account of how the island began:

> Asked during what period had men lived at Ravenser they say that forty years ago [it was more like sixty] a certain ship was cast away on Ravenser where there was no house then built, which ship a certain person appropriated to himself and from it made himself a cabin which he inhabited for some time, that there he received ships and merchants and sold them meat and drink, and afterwards others began to dwell there; and they say that thirty years ago there were no more than four houses.

This is an incredible story: it asserts that in sixty years, a small island developed on a shingle bank had become an important port, valued and rewarded by the King. It implies that a few individuals somehow gathered enough protection and cover to allow them to move from survival to marketing strategies over that generation. But over that generation, they had not only prospered but also held off the sea, and then, those in power had supported them as they were seen as a source of taxation and investment.

J.R. Boyle concludes from the report that nothing in it satisfied the Grimsby men. The result was that the case was heard by the King's Bench. This means that we have a good record of what was said there. Ravenser merchants had forestalled the trade and goods of chips headed for Grimsby: the charge was that they had 'violently arrested' the men bound for Grimsby, and that was against the established trading practices. Names were named:

> The aforesaid Walter and others on the Monday next before the feast of the Nativity in the first year of the reign of the present king [1273] arrested the aforesaid Lambert and others and compelled them to go to the town of Ravensrod and to harbour and sell their merchandise there and in this way have forestalled against the usage of the King's dominion.

It was all for nothing: the conclusion of the court was that 'the aforesaid mayor and commonalty of Grimsby gain nothing by their writ but are at the King's mercy for a false claim.'

Ravenser was providing well and earning its freedom to forestall. In 1296, pipe rolls record that fifty-eight sacks of Scottish wool were forfeited from there to the King. It was clearly well worth preserving, and the failure of Grimsby to change anything in the rivalry at the Humber mouth could only lead to further trouble. But Ravenser prospered. It really came into its importance in the wars between the Scots and Edward II.

In 1310, the King made preparations for an invasion of Scotland and he planned to assemble a fleet and an army, commanding his towns to raise resources. Ravenser was ordered to supply a warship and fighting men. In 1314, when he was fated to meet and be defeated by Robert the Bruce at Bannockburn, twenty-eight ports were ordered to supply ships and men, and again, Ravenser was included, and yet again in 1315, when Ravenser and other ports were commanded to apply a blockade on Scots trading on the coast. Also at this time the town was allowed to levy a tax to defend their walls. There were beginning to be signs of weakness in their position regarding the sea and the weather.

The first marked turning point, which was surely an event loaded with dread and foreboding, was in 1355, when bodies were washed out of their graves in the Ravenser chapel. Six years later, there were severe storms and floods. Sheppard summarizes the end of the town's existence, noting that divine punishment was involved, as he quoted in the Meaux chronicle:

But that town of Ravenserodd ... was an exceedingly famous borough, devoted to merchandise, as well as many fisheries, most abundantly furnished with ships and burgesses amongst the boroughs of that sea coast. But yet, with all inferior places, and chiefly by wrong-doing on the sea, by its wicked works and piracies, it provoketh the wrath of God against itself beyond measure. Wherefore, within the following few years, the said town, by those inundations of the sea and of the Humber, was destroyed to the foundations so that nothing of value was left.

Erosion had begun not long after 1300, and was evident again in 1346, the year of the Battle of Crecy. When Ravenser had contributed a ship to the expedition, two-thirds of the place was gone. In 1350, the chapel was ruined and the people were evacuated to Hull.

There is one place that is, without doubt, a community lost to the sea, or at least, a community that lost a great deal of its land: that was Meaux Abbey. In *Bulmer's Directory* for 1892, it was stated that the township of Meaux had 1,457 acres of land and seventy-six people living there; it was then merely a few scattered houses, a few miles away from the village of Wawne.

Meaux Abbey has figured largely in the story of Ravenser, and without the chronicle of Thomas Burton we would have very little information. His *Chronica Monasterii de Melsa* (published in English in 1906) documents the struggle of his own Cistercian monastery against the Humber tides, as well as the coastal confrontations with the power of the sea. The abbey was founded in 1151 by William Le Gros, positioned in a valley of the river Hull. Burton wrote his chronicle from 1496 to 1399, and during his time there was a fight to keep the water away. As a review of a study of Meaux points out, Thomas was caught up in the fight:

> The well-endowed monastery at Meaux had at this time [when the chronicle was written] lost valuable lands from the inundations of the sea and the Humber, and it was for the object or … under the pretext of repairing their permanent revenues, that a new abbot, Hugh of Leven, took measures for the appropriation of two neighbouring benefices.

Their beginnings were tough and interesting. The 1892 *Directory* gives the tale of the first phase of its life:

> Having resolved to fund a monastery for monks of the Cistercian Order, he [William Le Gros] communicated his intentions to Adam, a monk of Fountains Abbey, who was celebrated for his piety, his great architectural skill, and his refined taste and appreciation of the beautiful in nature. Adam … selected for his site an eminence in the beautiful but sequestered hamlet of Meaux. [The Earl of Albemarle] demurred to the choice of Adam and desired him to select some other plot … but the monk was inflexible in his resolution and, striking his staff into the

ground, he exclaimed with enthusiasm, 'This place shall in future be called the vineyard of Heaven and the gate of life and shall for ever be consecrated to religion and the service of God.'

The Earl gave way.

They had a tough life. In 1349, the plague took Hugh and forty of the fifty monks at the abbey. Over the century after about 1230, there had been a steady decline in the numbers of monks there: in 1249, there were sixty and in 1349, there were twenty-eight. In 1400, there was an inquisition of the abbey, and partly that was because the monks were suing for a reduction in rents to the Crown, as they had lost 27 acres since the 1330s. In the *Chronicles* of the abbey there are repeated entries logging the various attempts of the brothers to add banks to protect their fields, but repeated flooding was always too much for them and land was lost. If we need to have some idea of what happened when the Humber really flooded, this passage from John Mayhall's *Annals of Yorkshire* gives us the hard facts:

> The Humber, the Ouse and the Trent were visited by a tide of extraordinary height. There were 29 feet 8 inches of water at the Humber dock gates. Many parts of Hull were deeply flooded.... At Goole, the banks of the Ouse gave way in two places and hundreds of acres within 5 or 6 miles were speedily laid underwater.

Today, thanks to work done by the Humberside Archaeology Unit and others, some more knowledge of Meaux has been accrued; an aerial photograph of the earthworks there shows a very clear outline of settlement. It is now classified as one of the high status settlements, along with the Anglian monastery at Flixborough and St Chad's in Barrow-on-Humber.

Of all the towns, villages and smaller communities swept away and indicated on Sheppard's map of 1912, Ravenser (and its first existence as Ravenserodd) give us the most significant and knowable instance of what kind of communities these places would have been, and how they survived. In only a few cases is Sheppard wrong. For instance, he notes Sunthorpe as lost when in fact its outlines are still evident.

From the sea, the attention turns now to Holderness and to the locations gathering behind Spurn, or on the seaward side. The locations varied as different historians tried to place the locations. But whatever the actual positions of some of these villages, the search goes on for more knowledge of them.

Chapter 7

Lost and Reclaimed on the Humber

When I have seen the hungry ocean again
Advantage on the kingdom of the shore.

William Shakespeare, *Sonnet 64*

Creative writers of all kinds have responded to the appeal of Holderness for its unique wateriness. At the time of the last great serious flooding in Hull, Hessle and Cottingham, poet David Wheatley wrote, in an article on this area (where he worked at the time), '"Build your cities on the slopes of volcanoes," exhorted Nietszche, but in the absence of volcanoes the twelfth-century burghers of East Yorkshire settled on a floor of plain clay and silt instead.' That sums up the situation here very neatly.

Look at a current map of the Humber estuary and the dominant impression is that there is a great deal of mud. Looking from Spurn across the mud, it is a sight of a strange, static and dark sea in total contrast to the tides across the neck of land on which you stand, in wonder. A century ago, J.R. Boyle, in his very efficient and comprehensive survey of contemporary thinking about all that mud, tackled the question as to how it comes to be there. He began by avoiding stressing the positive: 'While this sediment is in some cases of value, and can be put to profit, at others it proves an unmitigated nuisance, and a continual source of anxiety.' He used a number of maps purporting to show the currents affecting the area, but reached no conclusion. Still, he was sure – and he was correct – that 'the mud in the Humber is accumulating.'

Counter to the drift of the narrative here, he pointed out that in 1912, there was new land:

It will be admitted that the mud in the Humber is accumulating. A most notable example is at Read's Island, between North and South Ferriby. Thirty years ago this was a comparatively small island, with a plot of grass in the centre in which a few cattle were reared. Now the island is hundreds of acres in extent, and has an enormous number of cattle grazing on it. In the neighbourhood of Spurn and Sunk Island, Broomfleet Island and in other parts of the Humber, acres upon acres of new land are continually being formed, while the Humber channel itself is almost choked with mud and sand.

In spite of Boyle's and others' calculations and studies of the rivers flowing into the Humber, and the attempts to understand the building and demolishing of land along Holderness, the end product is a massive area of mud, and to look across them, westwards, from Spurn, is to realize their extent. Between that tip of Spurn and the areas referred to by Boyle here, there is land reclaimed to counteract the lost land further north, but somewhere in that mud there lie the lost places. That thought invites the kind of melancholy meditation that the Augustan poets Gray and Collins tended to indulge in. With this in mind, a pause is needed to have a modern contemplation of this fascinating piece of Yorkshire, so often thoughtlessly overlooked.

Consequently, in the story of these coasts, it is an effort to imagine the nature of the communities in the area of Holderness south of Beverley. The general condition of the people's environment across the years is one of a watery landscape: low fields, plentiful waterways and mixed successes in efforts towards effective drainage are the overall features. The land, legally a wapentake and also a *seignory* (a manorial lordship) had owners ranging from the Crown to the Church, and to the more powerful characters such as the Sheriff of the shire or to wealthy families such as the Constables.

If some idea of the nature of the waterways around the homes in Holderness is needed, then studies of the havens of the Humber by Henry Irving are very useful. A perfect example is that of Broomfleet, about 4 miles west of Brough. Irving supplies a map that shows the complex mix of sands and muds alongside the locks and creeks of the area. The heart of this place is the entry of the Market Weighton Canal to the Humber sea wall. Irving defines this as 'a unique example of an eighteenth-century two-way self-acting sluice'. The map shows the human presence at Faxfleet Hall and at Broomfleet Farm, but along the bank there is Whitton Sand beyond the mud clinging to the shoreline. The case of Broomfleet makes it very clear that the settlements on the havens were trading and travelling in places where sandbanks created variable buoyage. Irving's comment for the visitor explains better than any number of facts the nature of this terrain: 'The visitor is advised to inspect the ground prior to arrival or to edge in early between the surrounding mud banks before they cover and create confusion.' Such has been the Holderness experience through the years, and those places that have gone forever must have lived with these dangerous relationships with the sea and the river.

For most, life there was a constant struggle. It has been remarked with reference to taxation and rent lists, just how many smallholdings there were: in many places, a house, a cow and a pig would be the basis of the economy, and fortunately, fish were always abundant. The note in the chapter on Spurn about the shortage of drinking water illustrates the toughness and deprivation of life on these coasts. Of course, the sea could sometimes have its own surprise bounty when wrecks meant that goods would arrive on the shore. The crime of wrecking (common in Cornwall, for instance) was rare on this coast, and the word 'wrecker' was usually used to mean a beachcomber. Christmas came early at Spurn in November 1895, when a steamer, the *Nantes*, was wrecked between Dimlington and Spurn Point. The Coastguard at Easington and Spurn were called out, but with little success. Then, as *The Shields Daily Gazette* reported, there was a feast for the locals:

> All the villagers were soon on the shore, and reaped a rich harvest from the waves. One 50-gallon cask of port wine first came ashore, followed by a similar one of methylated spirits … followed by sherry, pale and brown brandy … also by evidence that a Christmas cargo was coming up. Cases of currants, raisins, candied peel, tobacco pouches, brushes, soaps, candles, envelopes, writing paper … much to the joy of many a cottage wife and the children, who secured an early stock of Christmas toys, in the shape of the monkey-up-a-stick, dandy horse, dolls and the like. Many of these articles appeared to be little damaged by the waves.

The paper reported that the customs officers took charge of the alcohol. As to the broken steamer, it was blown up by the officers of Trinity House.

This organization has played an important part in the history of this coast, so it needs some explanation here. Its origins lie in the church community at Hessle, a little west from Hull, in 1169, when a group of locals formed a society that was for self-help. This eventually became a guild. When Hull developed (as Kingston-upon-Hull originally) throughout the fourteenth century, the churches of Holy Trinity and St Mary were central to its identity and its daily life.

The Guild arrived 200 years after the first small community in Hessle – in 1369. There were forty-nine men and women in that first group and they are listed in a document known as the 'First Subscription'. The organization provided help and support in time of need for all members, helped with funeral arrangements, and so on, much like the later Friendly Societies. Later, it founded the Hull Dock Company, and also other provisions for the coast, including the Coastguard. Its income up until the Dissolution of the Monasteries in Henry VIII's time, was partly from the land of the Carmelite friars.

One of its most important functions has been to manage alms houses, accommodation for needy seamen or widows of seafarers. Its later history played a considerable part in the management of the Holderness coast. The Guild members – called Brethren – were valuable as river pilots, for instance, and the House administrated such things as navigation tools, such as buoys. At Spurn, before the first lights, a hermit had taken on the task of maintaining some kind of light, and by the eighteenth century, as the summary in British History Online explains, Trinity House was important in the later provision:

Hull Trinity House continued to take an interest in the lighthouses, making requests and reports to the patentees, and giving them assistance. The failure of the patentees to carry out improvements eventually led to the Acts of 1766 and 1772, which provided that new lighthouses should be built under the direction of the London House [of Trinity].

By the early nineteenth century, Trinity House had control of the development of the Humber as pilot water; overall, it was an organization with great powers over navigation and coastal management.

What about the nature of the Holderness coast itself? Before looking at some of the lost villages, it is useful to look again at the basic geology. At the retreat of the ice sheet, described in chapter 1, about 10,000 years ago, what was left to form the terrain was boulder clay – a mix of silts and gravels. These are subject to rapid erosion, and this post-glacial material, known as *till*, is the stuff of those disintegrating cliffs. Where does the till go? It has been shown that it runs to Lincolnshire and into the Humber fringe and onto Spurn. The Hull Geological Society reports on the area suggest that in the future, Spurn will be an island again:

> It is currently being eroded and there will be a breaching of the spit … when the material that forms the spit at the Humber mouth grows too large for the mouth to support, the pressure of the water from the river and the wave action of the North Sea become too great for the loosely bonded material to hold back the incoming tides, which eventually breach it.

The map today shows massive mud areas, from the Skeffling clays off the Oxlands and Winsetts banks, down to the Easington Clays and then the Kilnsea Clays. Off these areas are the Trinity Sands, and this mud covers around 6 miles of shoreline from Kilnsea inland, out to about 6 square miles further out. On Sheppard's map of 1912, he marked Tharlesthorpe, Frismersk, Penisthorpe, Orwithfleet, Sunthorpe and Burstall Priory as being in this area. Underpinning his commentary on these lost places, we have the Meaux chronicle, referred to previously, as a useful source of events here.

Orwithfleet appears to have gone by 1339, destroyed by the Humber; Sheppard notes that Sir John of Meaux pressured the Meaux monks into payment for rented land of 33 acres of grassland there. Close by, Tharlesthorpe gave Meaux Abbey 300 quarters of grain, and Sheppard states that there were 1,274 sheep at Tharlesthorpe in 1277. There was also, in the thirteenth century, an area called 'The Green' there, and in the hard years of the 1340s, when plague and famine scourged the land, Sir Robert Constable took eight tofts [a piece of land where a toft or homestead had been] and four bovates of land from Tharlesthorpe. But as that century advanced, this village and the cluster of others of similar size began to lose value as well as land.

In this location, there is a place of special interest: Burstall, or Birstall Priory. The story of the place goes back to 1115, when Stephen, Earl of Albemarle, gave the land there to the Abbey of St Martin d'Auchy in Rouen. Monks came across and the community started. The chapel of St Helen built there was awarded income in tithes, from Skeffling nearby. The chaplain was given a moral role regarding the people of the area, apparently acting as a sort of spy on their behaviour. The first church courts must have been busy. Later, Richard II owned the Priory, and it appears that English monks replaced the French ones. Close to the end of the fourteenth century, the French abbey sold the Burstall set-up to Kirkstall Abbey, in Leeds – a very powerful brotherhood indeed, with plenty of land.

As one archaeological survey has put it, Burstall Priory now lies beneath the Humber mud, but that same report speculates on what lies there:

> The original St Helen's church may have been located here.... Somewhere nearby are presumably the buried remains of Burstall Garth, later Burstall Hall. This site was probably already in place in the medieval period, but the house described in 1650 as 'a strong stone building' may have been constructed from materials obtained from the Priory. It stood by the Humber edge by 1723, and had been demolished by 1765.

Something is known of the Priory, helped by a drawing used in Poulson's book on Holderness; he also adds that there is a known date of the first ordination there, in June 1219. The drawing, a woodcut, reveals three sides of a building, with a more solid part to the left showing two doors at the coastal side. There have been several archaeological finds there, including a Roman brooch, and Poulson gives a comment that Burstall generally must have been a populous place.

Of the other villages that were on the Humber coast, little is really known. Beresford included Penisthorpe in his listings, and he placed it to the west of Welwick; stray references to the village hint at what was there, such as a note on 'Green Close lying in Penisthorpe' from 1313, which Beresford quoted. He also extrapolated some details from such items as Lay Subsidies, and in 1377, for Penisthorpe and Welwickthorpe, the Poll Tax shows 107 taxpayers.

Beresford quotes the sad and significant fact that in 1525, only one tax payer in the two places 'met the taxable threshold'. By 1624, the reference to the village is not there, and Beresford concludes, 'By 1841, only small pieces of land still bear the name.'

Tharlesthorpe, lost and somewhere under the mudflats, as we know from the chronicle of Meaux, had a lot of work done to build new sea defences as early as the late 1390s, but it was destined to be swamped. Firsmersk, in contrast, which began to be flooded in the fourteenth century, again as recorded in the Meaux Chronicle, lost 321 acres during that same period, and this consisted of 100 acres of meadow and 152 acres of pasture.

In a calendar of papal registers for the 1370s, there is a very informative summary of the situation at Frismersk, along with a cluster of other manors regarding flooding:

> The Archbishop's letters ... make the same statements as above with respect to the manors of the Humber, giving them as follows: Tharbestorp, Witheflete, Dynelton and Revenserodd in Holdernesse; and with respect to the manor of Milton and of Hugeeston [Hull] ... they add also the towns of Ravenser, having been partially abandoned by its inhabitants on account of the desolation caused by the unwonted violence of the said inundations, the tithes and oblations arising from the chapel thereof, which depend on the recently appropriated church of Easington, have in large measure failed.

As usual, this is all in order to update the papal authorities and administrators regarding settled income and potential income.

For the communities once in these little places, we also have to look at the Roman settlement, and one or two of the locations have definite evidence of Roman occupation. Before Sheppard wrote in 1912, Dr Hewetson and then J.R. Mortimer had studied Easington, but by 1912, as Sheppard comments, the archaeological site was 'far out to sea'. The diggers found tumuli, and they were later lost; but pottery was found by a researcher called Stevenson, and the various finds both at Easington and at Spurn have related to a long-standing debate about where a place called by the geographer Ptolemy *Ocellum Promontorium* was Spurn or not.

In 1834, John Walker, of the Society of Antiquaries, wrote at great length in their journal, to show that Ptolemy's *Ocellum Promontorium* was Flamborough; he did this by also arguing that a place called Portus Felix was, in fact, Filey Bay. All that really matters is that there has certainly been Roman settlement along this coast, and it is obvious, for geographical and strategic reasons, that Flamborough, Filey Brigg and Spurn would have been settled and used, where possible at least for observational purposes, if not for landing. In fact, all three places, if used as signal stations, would be placed alongside (but further out to sea) wide bays where landings could indeed be made.

In Holderness, closer to the Humber side on the south, the villages and their history relate to the wider story of the battle with the water. The term 'wetlands' definitely applies, and visitors have not been impressed by the landscape in many cases. Daniel Defoe, for instance, in the 1720s, noted, 'The most that I find remarkable here is that there is nothing remarkable ... for above 30 miles together, not a port, not a gentleman's seat, not a town of note.'

There are geomorphological reasons for this: that is, explanations relating to land formation. These are basically fens. This whole expanse of Holderness is liable to flooding, either from the higher ground in North Yorkshire or from the Humber and Hull rivers threatening floods from the estuary. The land Defoe saw is therefore low, peaty and often underwater, even today. Within the last ten years, before 2016, there have been heavy floods at Hull, Hessle and Cottingham. The whole of East Yorkshire is consequently a landscape dominated by the network of canals and drains that have kept the area in business for a long time. But investment and hard work have to continue.

In past times, people were always aware of the richness of the resources there. There have always been shallower stretches with their retention of water, as well as the more wooded *carrs*, as they are called, which have depths of peat because the roots take up water and help retain earth. Although it is not actually in Holderness, Star Carr, near Scarborough, has been excavated and this has given us a good idea of the kinds of people who lived there back in the Mesolithic era. This is in the low vale of Pickering, and back in the Stone Age there would have been a string of lakes, and so the settlers would not only have had fishing, but they could also hunt the animals that came to drink.

As there has been a considerable placement of peat, the materials found in digs there have come up with such items as harpoon heads, bone workings and even amber, from the sea. Neil Oliver, in his study of early British history, summarizes the most impressive fi ndings: 'During the original 1950s excavations, Clark and his team recovered no fewer than twenty-one headdresses carefully fashioned from the skulls and antlers of red deer.' Pre-Roman life in Holderness is slowly and steadily being revealed and understood, and the water-centred cultures of the past, with the strategies for coping with the sea, are opening up to interpretation.

In more recent times, and up to the present, the outstanding feature of life there is the process of banking and dredging, cutting waterways and making canals – all tactics of coping with, and profiting from, the water. Ian Rotherham, historian of the wetlands, has pointed out just how much co-operation was needed across the population of the place. He explains what resources had been made, largely by workers for the religious houses:

> Bridlington Priory was an active reclaimer of these lands in the villages where it had ownership. By the thirteenth century too, Meaux Abbey was in dispute over fisheries at Hornsea Mere … fisheries were important at Wassand, Pidsea, where today the village remains the marker of the lost wetland. … There was also an eel pond at Brandesburton, the fishery of Eurmerske at Burstwick, and meres at Skipsea, Lambwath, Withernsea … all these have gone.

As to life with and by the extensive wetland terrain, it is interesting, as Ian Rotherham mentions in his book on the 'forgotten fenlands' of Yorkshire, a writer called Henry Strickland understood the importance of having landed gentry in one's province, and Strickland is quoted in writing about the gentry:

> Holderness, Harthill, and Ouse and Derwent, were full of the seats of nobility and gentry: a century ago … they possessed not fewer than eighty-nine mansion houses, and a century and a half before that, sixty-eight, where there now remain only forty-nine!

Strickland saw that the gentry were the ones who effected change, along with the abbeys; sure enough, in the 'Age of Reason', when people who owned land and halls felt the urge to 'improve' the look and function of their domain, things changed. Rotherham refers to Sir Joseph Ashe of Wawne, for instance, who started works to form a drainage network, and he used the technology of windmills to power the lowering of water levels.

The dwellers in the Holderness salt marshes, relying on drainage and embankments to protect their land, also lived with the accretion of mud. This was gradually forming land, and so there was reclamation, but the draining and pumping meant that the peat on the carrs would shrink. But as Rotherham points out, Hull was growing fast during the period when these problems were becoming acute for the landowners, and the river Hull was dredged, along with the raising of the river banks.

Rotherham sums up the situation at the end of the nineteenth century: 'The bulk of the waterscape of Holderness had gone and the farmland around it or which replaced it was intensively drained and under-drained.'

Still, there is the question of what the fight to retain land was like all along this coast. Here, specialists and experts help. Such a one is Jan Crowther, who has spent a long time understanding and analyzing Kilnsea and Spurn. Her A-Z of those places gives an insight into what lives and material cultures have existed and fought to exist there. The Spurn communities have partly been discussed, and in my next chapter there will be accounts of the railway and the military entrenchments there. But to round off the aspect of daily living in Kilnsea and Spurn, Jan Crowther's notes are essential. Her accounts of the families and settlers there help to give a picture of the lives in places that have, in many cases, gone forever.

For instance, places and families go hand in hand, such as the 'Walker Butts', which is a piece of pasture used until enclosure. Jan points out that this name came from a family called Walker who owned Southfield Farm back in the eighteenth century. The farm was auctioned in 1996 after the death of Arthur Clubley. Then there was Redvers Clubley, who had a field named after him.

The pub is so important in any community, and in this case, it was the Lifeboat Inn. Jan notes that when the row of lifeboat cottages was vacant in

1859, the end cottage, to the Humber side, became the pub. Before that, the locals drank at a pub in the coxswain's house, but this was washed away.

In the case of one particular building, there is a touch of humour. This is Appletree Cottage, also known as Mick's Place. Jan explains that this was made in the 1930s and was wooden. In the 1970s, the owner wanted to have a brick bungalow, but there followed a DIY catastrophe, when the entire place collapsed. Later, a caravan occupied the site, and then finally came another bungalow. There was also a bungalow belonging to a warden – Barry Spence, who started work there in 1964.

There were also, as will be seen, military occupations at Spurn and at the two Humber forts, in both world wars, and the oral history of those people gives us rare insights too, such as the memories of Bill Clarkson, who was there as a Territorial in the Second World War; he caught a glimpse of the lifeboat coxswain, Sam Cross, running out to the boat wearing only his underwear. Clarkson also saw a ship blown up nearby, and once again, out went the life-savers.

The lost communities, and those on the fringe who have fought to survive or struggled to do their daily work over the centuries, are open to our knowledge largely in fragments, oral history and scraps of memories; but those lives and places lost were integral to the broader communities, and so the context is important. If we take a typical example of a village close to so many actually on the shore – Patrington – it will be plain to see what a Holderness society has been. Patrington, only 18 miles from Hull, also nudges Patrington Haven, a hamlet just a mile away.

There was once a harbour there, but this shrunk to a creek; the star in its firmament is St Patrick's church, which gives the place its name. Back in 1820, its population was 1,244 and it had also a Methodist Meeting House and a chapel. The writer at that time commented that there were 'delightful views of the Humber and its fertile shores as far as Spurn Point, and the opposite shores of Lincolnshire render the prospect more beautiful.'

Although at that time the Haven was silting up, the famous Leeds newspaperman Edward Baines wrote that 'Several vessels trade to Hull and London.' Also, as well as farming, up until late the Victorian period, fishing was important there; the railway reached it in the 1850s. There were some grand buildings, such as the old rectory, built before 1700, and this even had a moated orchard; there was also a tithe barn, and from the tower of the church, as tourist guides tell you, the famous Captain Bligh surveyed the area.

At this point, the focus has to switch to the accretion of land: there has been land reclaimed, of course, on the Humber shoreline, and shifting sands move and in places gradually gather enough regained soil to be habitable. The perfect example is Sunk Island, which is now owned by the Crown estate, who have funded a £325,000 flood defence wall at Hawkins Point. They now own 11,400 acres of that area. This was done after the tidal surges of December 2013. This kind of activity has a long history, and Sunk Island itself has been involved in major history, in 1915, when a main gun battery was installed there for the defence of the Humber.

Sunk Island was described in a directory of 1892 as being a parish with 6,914 acres and a population of 440 then. The directory adds:

> The surface is level and monotonous; the soil, warp; and the subsoil sand and silt. A portion of the land is laid down in pasture, and on the rest, wheat, oats, beans and mustard are grown.... The whole parish is the property of the Crown, by whom new farmhouses and cottages were erected in 1854.

The sand and soil washed into the Humber is taken into the estuary, and what builds eventually is warp – river water with suspended sediment. This is a very effective fertilizer and was used as such on the Trent and the Humber by farmers, being brought in by sluice gates to flush farmland. At Sunk Island, there would at first have been a sandbank, then the warp would add substance and so there would be an island formed. In the seventeenth century, it had about 7 acres, and the channels running by it were deep enough to allow shipping. The man who bravely took on this tract as an investment was Colonel Anthony Gilby, who was Governor of Hull in 1668. He rented it for £5 a year.

Gilby struggled, and after some time he asked for help from the King. What he had was described as 'drowned land'. The land stayed with the Gilby family through the next century and more, and in the early nineteenth century, it was all opened up to new tenants. Success depended on embankments being built. The new community had the same problem as the monks of Meaux back in medieval times, but eventually, progress was made. A landmark in this progress was a road, described by the writer in the 1892 directory:

> In 1836, in consequence of representations made to the Commissioners of woods and Forests by the tenants and others, of the great inconvenience they sustained from the want of a carriage road ... an act was passed for making and maintaining a road from the church to the town of Ottringham, which was completed in 1841 at a cost of about £5,000. Other roads have been since constructed.

Matters progressed after that, with the building of a chapel and the creation of a parish with the name Sunk Island; in 1877, a new church was constructed, and what could have been more significant as a symbol of the renewal than a memorial window dedicated to the Reverend Robert Metcalf, who was the first incumbent of the parish? After that came a Methodist chapel and a school. A sandbank had become a parish.

In 1924, questions were asked in Parliament. The Minister of Agriculture was asked when the reclamation of land at Sunk Island was begun and to what use the land was put at that time. Of course, he also asked about income from the land, and it is interesting that Mr Buxton, the minister, had some impressive figures to hand:

> Mr Buxton: The most recent inclosure [*sic*] was in the year 1894. The total area of Sunk Island is approximately 10,500 acres, of which between 8,000 and 9,000 acres have been embanked and reclaimed in the last 200 years. The whole island is devoted to agriculture and is let as farms ... gross rental of £11,200 a year.

Chapter 8

Tales from Social History

They that go down to the sea in ships, that do business in great waters,
These see the works of the Lord, and his wonders in the deep.
The Book of Common Prayer

T he question must now be asked – what did these coastal communities do? How did they live? The answer is simple: the Yorkshire coast was all about fishing, smuggling, and as has been explained, iron ore and alum, but also it had always been rich in cultural life with expressions ranging from songs to fi shermen's jerseys. Religion was also strong, of course, and people died for their faith in great numbers during the Tudor period, down in Holderness, where they were kept in the Hull block houses and executed. Those villages and farms that have been swept away into oblivion were exactly like their surviving counterparts: fundamentally, they went fishing and they traded.

Added to this thought is the tantalizing footnote that tends to exist in the early literature, from the Viking raids of the AD 700s, onwards up to Domesday, in 1086. There was a Scandinavian culture in the settlements then, and the Vikings did indeed settle after the initial raiding period. The Old Norse word *Wintersetl* is used to describe that time when the warriors put down roots. A note in the *Anglo-Saxon Chronicle*, one of the major sources of information about the Saxon/Viking period, states simply that in 876, 'they shared out the land of the Northumbrians and they proceeded to plough and support themselves.' So very early in the Middle Ages then, there was a Viking culture of material richness. Today, the best way to understand that is, arguably, to visit York and experience the Jorvik Viking Centre, which is created on the site of what was an important Viking archaeological dig. York, naturally, was a key centre for the Roman, Viking and Norman civilizations, and when we look towards the coast from that centre, it is rational to expect investigations to find the same kinds of artefacts and the evidence for what life was like.

What went down under the waves was very much the same as what survives, and in a strange way, looking for the identity of those lost places is no different, superficially, to looking at villages that were different several hundred years ago. But that is not quite the case, because every community is at once both ordinary and unique. The question that must be posed is, how do we know any community from the past? The answer is that we know something of what has gone through work and play, beliefs and fears, rituals and fragmentary records. As the foregoing chapters show, the bare minimum in this respect is in the few facts written in the Domesday Book in 1086; after that, we have to rely on topics such as taxation and rents; where the power was exerted, there will be some kind of gain or loss, victory or defeat, and someone often makes a note of it.

If we can understand how these people worked and played, what they believed in and what stories they told, then we know what kind of communities were lost. Every time history or archaeology looks into the remains of the past, the artefacts, interesting in themselves, always lead to questions about the actual material facts of human life as it was lived at the time in question. This means that folklore tends to rub shoulders with hard-headed chronicles.

They were fishermen's villages. That meant that the basis of their work was a boat called a coble, a craft with a design based on the Viking long ship – broad across the middle and with a high stern and a long, finely-shaped prow. They were clinker-built, having overlapping planks for the cannily shaped boards and seams. The whole micro-economy of a village would have been made around the sail and the catch. But of course, there was a whole material culture around the daily life that was geared to successful fishing. The crafts involved fascinate the visitor; there are photographs showing holidaymakers in the 1950s gathering in curious crowds to watch with fascination the method of mending fishing nets; I can recall joining such a crowd on the coble landing at Filey in the late 1950s.

With the fishing came other maritime activities, and smuggling was one of them, intimately related to fishing or trading coal or iron ore. Trips were made along the coast and across the sea when cargo had been landed and there was space aboard, and history has shown that until the Victorian years, most forces worked with rather than against the lawbreakers. This was mainly because the powerful men who ran things were working with the smugglers – sometimes, even the magistracy was involved.

In the years between the first customs duties up to the 1850s, naturally, the hamlets and villages along this coast would have viewed smuggling as an accepted contribution to their economy and to their survival. The modern reader has to make an effort to envisage a world without social security and with very little official law and order. The markets were there across the sea in the early Middle Ages, at first with basic but valuable commodities such as stockfish and the herring catch. There was also a deeply entrenched communal self-help in the culture: through the period of most organized smuggling the law was harsh, so with the cruel sea on one side and repressive criminal law on the other, survival depended on the bonds of immediate society and family ties.

The historian of Yorkshire smuggling, Graham Smith, has provided one of the best accounts of why the illegal activities of smuggling were such an integral part of social life up to the mid-Victorian years:

> The impressive and dramatic nature of the coastline has largely dictated the type of free trade activities undertaken. Any study of smuggling throughout the country clearly shows that smugglers, if nothing else, were very skilful and resourceful in not only overcoming the natural features of their shores but also adept in using them to their best advantage.

Smuggling is such a major part of this history because, until the arrival of free trade and the removal of the burden of huge import duties on luxury goods in the 1840s, contraband handling was rife – it was part of the fabric of trade in many different forms. Smith makes it clear in his history of Yorkshire smuggling that the broad and sandy shores were ideal for the oldest, standard method – that of bringing the goods in onto the beach and into a cove or creek. The forces of law and order, ostensibly patrolling the coast, were in most cases outnumbered, or spread too thinly over their 'beat'. The men with the toughest task in this respect were the Riding Officers, who had to ride their stretch of coast, alone, and then when seeing any smuggling in progress, try to gather forces such as militia or customs men; if they tried to face out the villains, they were ruthlessly assaulted and sometimes killed.

In Holderness, an important strand of the social history was indeed political. By the sixteenth century, Hull was a very important port, with trade and transport extending across the world. It was no accident that Henry VIII's government, in the suppression of Catholicism, made the port a stronghold; even more than that, it made it a prison – or rather a string of prisons. These were the block houses to the east of the docks: fortified jails in a group of towers. Here the recusants – in many cases, the priests who insisted on saying mass or writing in favour of the 'old religion' – were held and often put to death.

In the context, a small settlement in Holderness has a link to the mainstream of history. This is the story of the Wright family, who had a branch at Plowland Hall, and they had land at Penisthorpe, Welwick and Thorpe Garth. Penisthorpe, as has been explained, was lost to the sea and is on Sheppard's map of 1912; now, family history research has shown that William and Ann Wright, of Plowland, whose memorial in brass is in St Mary's, Welwick, relate to John and Christopher Wright (stepbrothers of William). These two went to St Peter's School in York, where they met Guy Fawkes and became radicalized. There was even a barn at Welwick called Plotters' Barn.

Writing their family history, Daniel Wright and David Herber explain the connection of the two brothers to the Gunpowder Plot:

> John is occasionally referred to as 'John Wright of Twigsmore', a manorial estate in the parish of Manton, Lincolnshire, owned in the latter part of the sixteenth century by the Tyrwhitt family, ex-school colleagues of Guy Fawkes and the priest Oswald Tesimond, and tied by marriage to the Percys of Spofforth. This completes the picture of these two young men and helps us in understanding how they became involved in Catesby's plot to kill James I.

In his book on the block houses, written in 1913, Joseph Hirst gives a full account of the unfortunate people whose fate was to be imprisoned in them. Many were from Yorkshire, and a typical victim from quite nearby was William Andleby, from Etton, just 4 miles north-west of Beverley. He was ordained in Europe and sent on the English missions. He had travelled Yorkshire on foot, 'meanly attired, and carrying with him, usually in a bag, all his belongings, for his labours lay chiefly among the poor.' His fate was to be hanged, drawn and quartered.

But in spite of all these various aspects of the lives and material culture around the Holderness and East Yorkshire people, there are some periods in the social history of the coasts that highlight the ordeals of living against the sea perhaps more vividly than others. These have been, over the years, industrial workers, the Coastguard, lifeboat men, churchmen and teachers, together with the military personnel, as the latter have always been a certain element in the populations of these places. Once again, Kilnsea and Spurn provide the clearest examples.

If we needed a typical community in this context, it would be outstandingly the workers on Spurn, and the perfect case study is the railway. This was built in 1915 and closed in 1951; arguably, the formidable site of Spurn is the last place one would expect a railway to be established. But its arrival related to the advent of the Great War in 1914, and Spurn was to be a key location in the defence and supervision of the east coast against attack from the sea and from the air, as the new threat of the Zeppelin air balloons came with the war. In fact, these fiendish creations did attack Whitby, Scarborough and Hartlepool, and also Cleethorpes, in December 1914.

Spurn was fortified in both world wars, and there was a railway there, being ready for work in 1915, but again, the reason for this was initially military. Ron Freethy, who has written about the 'secret war' in Yorkshire during both world conflicts, used a fascinating element of oral history in his research, and his interview with Nigel Woods opened up a rare insight into the use being made of Spurn:

It turned out that detailed plans had been made as the long beach at Spurn Head down to the lighthouse was expected to be a German point of landing.... A new road was being built, there were pillboxes everywhere, and huge concrete blocks so that they acted to deter the movement of tanks.

This was to be at the tail end of its military use, but back in 1915, it was crucially important to east coast defence and the railway played an important part in the history.

Spurn was known in 1914 as the Godwin Battery, and that extended to Kilnsea and environs too; in addition, there were the two island forts, which have been described very vividly by Ken Hartley in his book on the railway:

> The two island forts were very substantial affairs built largely of concrete. For about half its circumference, the Bull Sand fort had on its seaward side a cladding of armour plate 1 foot thick, outside a 3-foot thick reinforced concrete wall backed by a ¾-inch thick steel plate. The Humber side was composed of concrete 2 feet thick enclosed by a ¾-inch steel plate; this was also the case with the shore side of Haile Sand fort ... accommodation was provided for some 200 persons on Bull Sand and 120 on Haile Sand.

Spurn itself at that time was fortified, and the work was done by C.J. Wills, a contractor from Manchester. The decision to build a railway rather than a new road is an interesting one and Ken Hartley puts the reason down to the wide availability of stock. It was first used to carry the building materials for the new wall, and then for a variety of military reasons. Ken Hartley's book gives a very accurate notion of what was built at that time and what kind of community worked and lived there. The railway work entailed a jetty, sheds, a workshop, and other accommodation. At the time of the Great War, there was still the Lifeboat Inn, and a passenger platform was made there. On a map of that time, there is a clear indication of the buildings across the whole Head: at Kilnsea, a hospital and barracks; an officers' mess; a rocket post and inn by the Easington Road; the railway buildings, and the lighthouse cluster, with associated dwellings.

Between the wars, the railway had all kinds of uses, and photographs show that there was what might be called a crowd boarding the train at the Old Fort. Functionally, the line took supplies up the Head, for the Humber forts as well as for the Spurn dwellers; but of course, when it comes to the British and a railway line, there are many social uses. Ken Hartley explains:

It was not unknown for the somewhat rare visitors of the 1920s to unofficially make this rail journey.... One on occasion, in the 1924–27 period, an enterprising charabanc proprietor ... advertised 'an excursion to Kilnsea with a train ride to Spurn'. The notice ... was displayed in the centre of Hull, where unfortunately, it attracted the attention of the military 'top brass'.

The local entrepreneur was in trouble and it never materialized.

Also in the years before the Second World War, Spurn operations became the domain of the Royal Engineer Civilian employees, and by 1939, this proved to be the base work for an anti-aircraft gun emplacement. At that time, as Ken Hartley wrote, the families and servicemen living there had a hard time still, but things took a step towards modernization:

By the latter part of 1932 ... the houses had been equipped with water-borne sewage disposal ...meat and provisions were brought out once a week from Easington by horse and cart.... Lighting was by oil lamps, for there was no gas or electricity supply, but fuel for fires was no problem – there was always ample driftwood to be found on the shore.

There was also free sea coal. A photograph from the 1930s shows the lifeboat crew carrying baskets, collecting sea coal, ably assisted by the crew's pet dog.

What was done in the leisure time, one might ask. There was always swimming and fishing, of course, but also there was a tennis court that had been constructed by the army, and there was gardening; for the evenings, there might not have been dance halls, but there was the radio and the Light Programme.

In the 1939–45 conflict, the Spurn guns were updated, and the same was done on the Humber forts. This entailed a new road as well, being built from the Blue Bell at Kilnsea, with the necessary passing bays. The defence installations were visited by Princess Mary in 1940, and she was carried in the Hardy railcar. She had to walk on a plank to exit because the driver overshot the platform.

Of course, erosion and sea damage went on. During the war, the seaward banking for the railway disappeared with a high tide, and as Ken Hartley puts it, '30 yards of track was left suspended in the air.'

So far in this chapter, there has been a survey of the major events that underpinned life in these lost or threatened places – wars, smuggling, religious strife, social dissent and so on. But there is also the cultural life, the very identity of these villages. They were close-knit, self-help, family structured clusters of homes, and the fact that they were so constantly threatened by destruction from the sea by gales or erosion means that looking at them today, with a need to understand their social history, is a search into the minutiae of life. Glimpses into that way of life come in snatches, from memoirs, interviews, press reports and even from folklore and storytelling, songs or dancing. A typical, and very valuable instance of this is found in a newspaper feature by an anonymous writer in 1928, headed 'Jersey Knitters of Flamborough'. What the writer does is far more than explain the knitting of the 'gansey' – the distinctive woollen jumper of the fishermen knitted by their wives – and he offers an account of the whole community.

He meets and speaks to half a dozen men and women of Flamborough, and his scene-setting gives a documentary image of the home and people, starting with a domestic interior and then moving on to this:

Years ago, the women would go up and down the steep slope at the North Landing in charge of the nimble-footed little donkeys which carried the bait or the catch or the crab pots.... Each woman wore a black sun bonnet, a black apron and a short skirt. Stout boots on her feet, and tucked away under one arm, the jersey she was knitting. Her two hands would be occupied with the long, twinkling needles, which flashed under her deft fingers.

Then the writer offers a slice of history for us, embedded in a little house:

Miss Eleanor Major lived in High Street ... a big woman, this, who could not show me her knitting, as it had just been sent home in the shape of a mauve golfing pullover. 'I can show you a jersey, though. Father has got it on,' ... so into the kitchen we went. There sat the most cheerful sea rover, in blue jersey, blue trousers and with bright, twinkling blue eyes. ... Soon we were yarning away like old friends and the wartime tales of battle, murder and sudden death, of which he had been an eye witness, were hair raising to say the least. As befitted a man whose great uncle – 'Traf' Cammish of Filey – had fought under Nelson at Trafalgar.

There were also other commercial activities, marginal, but intrinsic to the life on the coast. A typical instance of this was the collection of eggs from the cliffs. Bempton is the spot where this was such a tempting business proposition for many, if they had the courage to swing across the precipices and venture towards the nests. It was certainly a formidable place to work. Thomas Pennant wrote, in the late eighteenth century, 'In some places, the rocks are insulated, are of a pyramidical figure and soar up to a vast height; the bases of most are solid, but in some places pierced and arched.'

W.R. Mitchell, writing more recently, explains what the situation was like, by referring to a directory of 1831:

This ... referred ... without sense of guilt to raids conducted on auk's eggs, which were collected in bushels and taken to the sugar house at Hull. Crowds attended Flamborough Fair, held on Whit Tuesday, and 'sportsmen' fired into the ranks of birds, continuing the carnage at lower levels firing from boats. The poorest shot was guaranteed to kill. Thousands of kittiwakes were killed so that their feathers could adorn ladies' hats. A distaste over such activities led some prominent East Yorkshiremen to steer through Parliament a Seabirds' Preservation Act; after much discussion, the Royal assent was given in June, 1869.

From long back in time, farmers who had land on the clifftops had a right to collect eggs, and they were known as 'climmers'. There are old photographs of these men, in baskets or with ropes, assailing the nests, and using various crafty ploys to rid the nests of the adult birds' protection. In a 1930s' travel guide, there is a photograph of climmers and a description of their skills:

The further the descent is made, the greater the motion, and the climber is frequently suspended in mid-air many feet away from the cliff. The eggs are snatched off the ledges as the climber swings up to the face of the cliff.

A Mr W.J. Clarke of Scarborough told the author of the same guide, with heart-stopping visual explanation, 'The climber wears round his waist a stout leather strap, to which are attached two pieces of webbing passing round the thighs from back to front. To this are fastened two iron eyelets, through which the rope is knotted.'

There is also the insight provided by crime. In the court records we have fascinating asides on the everyday lives of these sea coast families. Regarding Skipsea, for instance, Roy Kirke has written a comprehensive account of the spectrum of the law as it was manifest in the various institutions and power structures through the centuries, ranging from the church courts to manorial courts and trials for serious crime. One topic here that really gives an insight into life and its pressures is the payment of tithes. A tithe was a payment, a tenth in most cases, made to the churchmen out of earnings, so they were payment in kind, and of course, widely hated. Because the tithes were paid from such everyday possessions and products as wood, grain, eggs or livestock, the nature of life is opened up for us. Roy Kirke gives a typical example: a certain Ralph Bainton, of Skipsea, who, in 1679, was taken to court because he had not paid tithes on 'goslings, chickens, young turkeys, hewn eggs or turkey eggs'. He was forced to pay.

Accounts of smuggling incidents also provide useful insights. In terms of confirming the view that these communities were tightly knit and carried out their own actions in interference of the law, one of the significant cases – that of the murder of James Law in 1823 – gives a very clear view of this. Law had come to Mead's home to threaten him and disturb him, with some friends, and Mead shot him dead. The backstory was that Mead was a paid informer of the Crown and he had informed on Law some time before. The hatred and need for a vendetta was palpable for all in the area. Historian Peter Howarth, in his detailed account of the case (which ended with the trial and conviction of Mead at York, and so his appointment at the gallows) gives a particular mention of one incident:

There were other violent disturbances. The house of Maw, the Revenue Officer, was stoned. There was a riot at Burniston and more violence in Scarborough that led to magistrates swearing in seventeen Special Constables.... 1,500 people attended Law's burial and to hear the verses of the derogatory song about William Mead sung over the grave.

What this makes very plain is that there was in these communities an invisible but entrenched moral law – a way of sorting things out locally – and this was often at odds with the criminal law itself.

Then there are the myths and legends: these always figure in social and cultural history. According to some folklorists, there is Britain's own 'Bermuda Triangle' to be found within an area known as Wold Newton, extending from a little inland from Scarborough down to Flamborough Head in the south, and then across to a few miles west of Burton Agnes. The triangle allegedly runs into an area of the North Sea. One theory is that this relates to the settings of the worship of stone monoliths in prehistoric times, with such evidence as animal masks (as found at Star Carr) being invoked. But strangely, the area also borders on the odd sightings made on the Barmston Drain just south of Bridlington, where a supposed werewolf known in the East Riding as Old Stinker has often been seen, most recently in 2015, by a number of local people.

These mythical and even paranormal tales can hardly be ignored: the Yorkshire coast is a place that has a history in which recorded factual records and documents stand side by side with the songs, oral tales and folk traditions that always seem to be rich wherever the sea is in proximity to human settlements. It is surprising that myths of a 'Yorkshire Atlantis' have not been concocted, given the series of defeats to the power of the sea.

Within the Wold Newton area there is also the 'gypsey race', which is a stream (nothing to do with gypsies) that has its source at Wharram and eventually runs into Bridlington harbour. The name comes from the Old English *gypsia*, meaning a spring; there is also the Greek word *gupos*, which refers to a chalk spring. The gypsey race can run underground and then appear again, above ground. One local tale is that it floods before any significant national event.

So many of the myths and folk tales of the area relate to water and the sea: the one that most closely relates to the lost places is the Owthorne story of the 'Sister Churches'. This story is given in the Reverend Thomas Parkinson's book of 1889, *Yorkshire Legends and Traditions*:

On the east coast of Yorkshire, about 14 miles from Hull, there stood two churches in close proximity to each other – St Mary's Church, Withernsea, and St Peter's, Owthorne, and known as the 'Sister Churches'. A tradition accounts for their having been erected so near together. Two ladies, sisters, determined to build a church for their tenantry, and fixed upon Owthorne for their site. The edifice was completed all but the tower or steeple. A dispute then arose between the ladies, as to whether the church should have a tower only, or the tower should be surmounted by a spire. So bitter grew the contention, that their friends persuaded them to submit the dispute to the Abbot of Kirkstall for settlement ... who, finding no other means of satisfying both ladies, decided that each of them should build her own church, after her own taste. This they did. Owthorne being already appropriated to the one, the other chose Withernsea, and there erected the sister church. For many years they thus existed, most acceptable landmarks to the sailors on the coast, who always spoke of them as 'Sister Churches'.

The fate of the two churches plays a part in the chronicle of losses in this book. A directory of the 1820s has this note:

This village, situated on the shore of the German Ocean, has suffered much from the encroachments of the sea, which are averaged at from 1 to 2½ yards annually along the coast. The church dedicated to St Peter ... on the night of 16 February 1816, fell with a most tremendous crash into the bosom of the ocean.

A very old church – St Mary's, going back to 1448 – was ruinous in the Regency period and was eventually replaced. The bits of bare records repeatedly show the importance of the church building (and position) in understanding what was once a hamlet or a village, and they became the caretakers of memorabilia as well as memorials.

Owthorne has been briefly described in chapter 4. The story of the sisters and the churches is entirely in keeping with the stories and legends concerning water and the sea; it comes as no surprise to learn that one of the very oldest tales relates largely to a hero giant called Wade, whose tales go back to the twelfth century at least, in a work by Walter Map, who describes him as 'a huge man with sprinkling grey hairs'. In the thirteenth century, Wade appears in the *Thithreks Saga* from Norway, and in that he is a son of a sea giantess.

Although Wade crops up in tales around Mulgrave and Goldsborough, it is the notion of Wade's Boat that dominates the legends. Wade, the hero, is supposed to have had a wonderful boat, although the source of the tales is not known. Westwood and Simpson, in their comprehensive folklore survey *The Lore of the Land*, express the uncertainty:

> Whatever this tale of Wade was, it was still known at the end of the sixteenth century.... Scholars conclude that Wade was originally a sea giant from the Baltic region, stories of whom were brought to England by the first Anglo-Saxon settlers.

This folklore has been inextricably mixed with the social and cultural history, as it always tends to be. It makes complete sense that tales of sea voyages and mythical seamen would filter into such stories in this area. At the moment, in many of these, the sources point in the direction of Scandinavia. It is impossible to overlook or underestimate the heritage of the Vikings and the Romans; finds at digs keep on adding to our knowledge, at least in the material culture. But there is always the impossible dream, such as one archaeologist who said to me, 'What we need is a human fossil ... where do you find those then?' He was joking.

Perhaps the only really satisfying way to understand that social history from the string of villages and chapels, barns and signal stations is to use the arts to recreate that past experience. In the last twenty years, there has been a generally renewed interest in the working communities of the past, as oral history has mixed with film and drama. If this is not done, then the eighteenth-century places will be as remote from our understanding as the prehistoric sites in that seabed that was once Doggerland. The next best thing is to make reconstructions, such as has been done at the museum in Dunwich, Suffolk, where the old Dunwich was lost to the sea. The curator has painstakingly built a model of Dunwich, taken from the written records. Visitors now see a large, detailed scale model of a township as it was before the sea destroyed it.

There are attempts made to access the memories in this context, such as local history groups gathering material from people. There is also some research on this, exemplified partly by Stephen Friend's University of Hull thesis on 'A Sense of Belonging' on this coast. Friend picks up on one of the themes in this chapter: the everyday work and the paranormal or mythical. He writes, 'The roles of women were many and various, including responsibility for the more mundane activities ... such as dress, ganseys and rag rugs ... although these were imbued with magical and superstitious properties.' Again, it is the textless history that is needed, largely through oral history projects, if we are ever to move closer to knowing more about those villages.

In a sense, Yorkshire has a place that is arguably in the process of joining Dunwich and Ravenser: Port Mulgrave. Today, it is as if watching the little port is an act of witnessing a gradual dissolution. At least, because there was an industry there, its story partially entered the records of written history.

Chapter 9

Conclusions

Yesterday it was a somewhat unusual high tide, and I stood about an hour on the cliffs ... watching the tumbling of great tawny turbid waves that made the whole shore white with foam.

Charlotte Brontë, *Letter to her father, 1852*

Charlotte Brontë's letter home was written soon after the death of her sister, Anne, in Scarborough. Perhaps she found consolation in staring at the sea. Certainly, in keeping with the Romantic writers and artists of her time, she found that the essential sense of wonder that mankind hungers for is reliably there on this always interesting coastline. The future of the place seems to be assured in this sense: it will be a very long time before the cliffs and tides stop being mesmeric, and the beachcombers and fossil hunters may go on thanking the forces of erosion for laying bare the treasures they seek. Nevertheless, this coast still has people on it, clinging to their livelihoods.

A subject concerned with disappeared and disappearing land can hardly be expected to draw optimistic conclusions. The fact is that a study of the history of this coast, from Scarborough down to the Sunk Island, can only be a catalogue of loss. Yet, as the Kilnsea community have shown, there may be regeneration. The case of Spurn comes to mind immediately in this context, as it has in the last half-century shown resilience and has re-invented itself.

When Andrew Gallon wrote about Spurn in early 2016 for *The Dalesman*, he travelled along the spit with Andy Mason, the heritage officer for the Yorkshire Wildlife Trust, and Gallon's perspective was one of bright enjoyment, with no shade of a lament for past depredations. He had a right to be: £600,000 has just been spent on preserving the lighthouse, but nevertheless, a reference is made to the lost community, which was discussed in my chapter on Spurn: 'Spurn was quite a community ... that's all gone now but we tell the stories of those who lived here: the seven lifeboat families, the Coastguard and the lighthouse keepers.' Still, the usual awareness of what lies beneath never quite goes away on a visit to Spurn, and Gallon notes that somewhere, with location unknown, beneath them as they walked, lies a gun emplacement.

But the spirit of Gallon's report is one that looks to the future. 'Yorkshire Wildlife Trust has further impressive plans for Spurn. Thanks to a £390,000 award from energy supplier EON, which operates the Humber Gateway offshore wind farm, it aims to open by April 2017, a purpose-built visitor centre.'

However, in tracing the progress of the erosion on this coast over the last century, it has to be said that reports, protests and complaints have kept on being repeated. In 1947, for instance, in the autumn, just before that particularly savage winter, fifty members of the North Eastern Centre for Sanitary Inspectors' Association inspected the coast at Hornsea Burton. An engineer-surveyor, Mr H. Wilkinson, gave a paper on the findings, and the press reported:

Along the Holderness coast from Flamborough to Spurn, the sea was eating into the land at a faster rate than almost anywhere else in the country.... Mr Wilkinson commented that the government must approach the problem of coast erosion in a new light and if agricultural land, houses and villages were to be preserved, the financial burden must be spread over a wider area than the immediate local authority.

He saw a new scheme for defence as a 'practical proposition'.

Three years later, the Skeffling Drainage Board sent a letter to Holderness Rural Council concerning the protection of Long Bank by Skeffling. The letter asked that the army be used to rebuild that sea defence. The response of the Holderness Council was that Councillor Connor, according to the *Hull Daily Mail*, 'did not like the tone' of the letter. Connor told the press, 'I can see a lot of trouble coming from coast protection.' The people at Skeffling must have been furious and frustrated.

This example encapsulates the nature of the to and fro of opinion, reportage and financial unease that have always lain at the heart of any move to really protect and maintain this coast. The fight goes on to conserve and protect. As I write this in August 2016, the news from Broomhill Sands Shore, in East Sussex, is that 250,000 tons of rock, brought from Norway, are to be placed there. This is happening as Brigitte Bass, a member of Defend Our Coast, is facing the loss of her clifftop home. Help seems to have arrived in the nick of time, and people in East Yorkshire must be envious.

It seems fitting to end with a distant, objective view of this history of doomed communities. It is hard to resist the temptation to take an elegiac tone here. The chronicle of events on this coast, from earliest times, has been one that itemizes one disaster after another, and the newspaper archives provide a constant stream of shipwreck reports and crews lost to Davy Jones's Locker. Over all this business and trade, over the raising of families and the scratching out a life from the harvest of the sea or the few fields of a coastal farm, there remains the elegy to the people and to the places. Spend a few hours walking anywhere on those crumbling cliffs, preferably below at the sand level, and it is impossible to ignore the sense of history, as pressing on the present as a face in a soft pillow.

Walking the promenades of the successful and thriving resorts, there is no imminent threat to any sense of security; all is prosperous and the crowds amble by with their ice creams and desultory chatter. But behind all the summer strolling and leisure, there is this long, aching history of loss. My book has provided place after place as doomed communities, from villages down to isolated houses or chapels; but in fact, over the apparently fragmented families and farms there is a communal experience, and it runs deep. This is why Kilnsea's story is so powerful: because it has been reinvented, reasserted. In 1835, George Head saw and wrote about the quintessential 'lost to the sea' experience, and he described it with all the passion and style of an age that was fascinated by what it called 'the picturesque'. As we read his account of this victory of the sea, it is as well to recall that this was written in an age when wealthy gentry were likely to employ a 'hermit' to adorn their grounds: a ruin of humanity amid the ruins of stone. Head wrote, as he approached Kilnsea:

> On arriving at this spot, I saw indeed the most extraordinary spectacle, and to the greatest advantage, inasmuch as the tide had not yet sufficiently

risen to prevent a free passage along the seashore below the cliff. In one large mound lay piled to a considerable height, the ruins of the church; large masses of the walls adhering closely cemented together, as well as fragments of the round spire; the latest avalanches of earth, consisting of rich churchyard mould, in which were profusely scattered bones, skulls, fragments of coffins, remnants of garments, buttons etc., were heaped in some places under the edge of the cliff, in height almost level with the summit. Already had the sea taken to itself the sacred edifice, and now the waves were tearing the churchyard fast away.

What really impressed Mr Head very profoundly was the sight of skeletons with silk handkerchiefs around their necks. In common with the many educated travellers of his generation, he was educated in the 'still life' composition available to artists in nature. The debate about art being subservient to nature had been discussed in the academies and in the literary press for some time. Artists and writer had been setting out to discover England's hidden places, particularly after the impressive success of Wordsworth in backing up the painter's depiction of wild nature in the Lakes. Here, in Holderness, was an instance of nature showing how small and pathetic were the tiny creatures labelled mankind. What Head saw would have confirmed the theory that God's divine creation was something He controlled and we simply managed as best we could in the face of it.

This line of thought sits uneasily with the advance of the culture of technology the advanced world has seen and backed since the first steam engine and Stephenson's *Rocket*. Generally, to the Victorians who were gathering sufficient faith in technology to think that machines could triumph over nature, the sea presented a problem. It had repeatedly stopped expeditions such as Franklin's fated journey to find the North West Passage in 1845, and it tended to cause such horrors as those delineated by Coleridge's *Ancient Mariner*.

Because the sea and the shore were widespread metaphors for such things as faith and love, death and hope, the images and experiences of a threatening sea could conjure any number of feelings to the Victorians. In Matthew Arnold's poem *Dover Beach*, of 1867, for instance, there is no doubt that a tide rarely brings anything near an optimistic mood:

Listen! You hear the grating roar
Of pebbles which the waves draw back, and fling
At their return, up the high strand,
Begin, and cease, and then begin again,
With tremulous cadence slow, and bring
The eternal note of sadness in.

Of course, the sea was, and surely still is, a distinctively profound element in the British psyche; a nation of mariners has always been part of our definition, and we are as much a nation of watchers of the sea as well as players and workers on the sea. With all that in mind, so the thinking has always gone, we should be able to master the sea. But there it is, eating away our green and pleasant land.

One lesson from this history is that, of course, the sea is creating as well as destroying: the drag of the destructive waves in their backwash does deposit and then shift, with the tide's flow, stone and sand to another place. There are 'rules' of geomorphology – the shaping of land and water as it moves, wears away, builds up, and so on. But in terms of human community, there is no consolation in this. People have stood and watched, helplessly, as land is devoured.

Yet more optimistically, geology has advanced so far that there is now a deeper understanding of coastal erosion, and together with marine archaeology, this science will gradually develop strategies for defences that will be more and more successful. Of course, there is another factor, and this has been an influence through history: the tendency of mankind to do foolish and thoughtless things such as exploitation of resources without too much thought. Phil Mathison, an expert on Spurn and the surrounding area, has written about the extraction of gravel and cobbles from Spurn. When this began, the land was owned by the Constable family of Burton Constable Hall, and there was a good profit to be made, as these materials were used in the construction industry. But of course, this kind of industry would have a major effect on the process of erosion. Not until 1925 was the Spurn area taken over by the government, and so the business came to a stop.

The human involvement with the landscape of the coast has rarely been such that it would be deleterious to the retention of land; the Spurn instance is thankfully rare. But every year there is some kind of controversy on the coast, and as I write this, the plans to build a massive wind farm 6 miles off Bempton Cliffs is completely at odds with the aims of the RSPB, who are maintaining the bird sanctuary on those cliffs. The oppositions and debates go on; such is the beauty and grandeur of those coasts from Redcar down to Spurn Head.

The debate as to what should be done goes on and on. A significant stage in this was in 1995, when Professor John Pethwick of Hull University spoke to the website Coastview, concerning the Yorkshire East Coast, and his words would not have been any kind of consolation to the farmers whose ancestors' places were rubble on the sea floor. He said:

These problems are chiefly about the movement of sand from north to south by the tides. The presence of sand acts as a natural barrier and helps to slow the process of erosion. But manmade sea defences get in the way of the sand's natural movement southwards, so deprived of sand, the shore immediately to the south of sea defences will erode more quickly.

Even more unwelcome would have been the words of the then Spurn Heritage Coast officer, Tim Collins:

These defences were not a good idea for the area generally. I know people get terribly worked up when they see the cliff edge disappearing into the sea, but hard defences in one place only result in more erosion in another place.

It would be easy to say that history teaches us that there are always winners and losers, and Professor Pethwick clearly does not own a property on the edge of land at Skipsea. It is not difficult to make theoretical comments about what erosion does when there is no sea waiting to invade your dining room. History also teaches us that the victory is not always to the strong – it is often to the fortunate. It is impossible to resist the thought that had other landowners acted as Mr Strickland did at Owthorne, some of the villages and farms that melted away might still be there.

From the start, this book was conceived as in part a work of archaeology of a kind – verbal rather than material. Digging for substance in the fragments of narratives concerning all those lost homes and churches was always going to be a history of the vestiges of places rather than anything of definite establishment in this coastal landscape. Yet, at least those lost places have something in common: a shared history of marginalization. Even when the railways came, late in the nineteenth century, places such as Out Newton or Cowden, Kilnsea or Old Aldbrough were still border settlements, and they had been since Roman times.

This coast was always beyond the pale in terms of the centres of civilization. If Aldborough is considered, for instance – the Roman administrative settlement, not the coastal Aldborough – the situation regarding the signals stations was one of a real focus of a working population of invaders, in contrast with the *ultima thule* of the cliffs and bays open to the great ocean of the geography, Ptolemy.

My most assured conclusion is that my initial vision of another Yorkshire, one there once upon a time in green fields, busy hamlets, and fisher folk at the nest, is still there, but whereas I began with a poetic and fanciful notion that there was a Tyke Atlantis out there, layered over the ancient Doggerland of carboniferous rock and fossil-packed sediments, changed to the hard-headed realization that these lost places now exist in atomized vestiges, part of mud flats and shingle drifts around the Humber and Lincolnshire.

In December 2013, there was a tidal surge that overwhelmed much of Spurn; yet, there was recovery. It was a case of all hands to the pump, as the debris from the Humber washed over the warren and the main area of the headland. Watchers saw litter mixed with mud and stone – something that people in years gone by would not have seen. That has been the pattern of assault and response through history, and all that may be said is that some places went under and some battled on. There is always a value in optimism – perhaps informed by science.

In terms of knowing more about what lies under mud and soil, notably in Holderness, the future is bright; archaeological studies make full use of aerial photography and of geophysical approaches. Documentaries continue to be made on lost places beneath soil, sand and water. As has been shown in the story of Sunk Island, for instance, land grows as well as shrinks. Yet even the very name 'Sunk Island' suggests a tale of loss and erasure.

The fascination and mystery involved in trying to consider and envisage the people and lives of the villages lost to the sea are in marked contrast to the other lost villages within the mainland. In Yorkshire, for instance, we have the example of the village of West End, which was submerged in 1966. It was a village in the Washburn Valley, and the water that now covers it is the Thruscross Dam. With West End, we know what is under that water. John Burland, writing in *The Dalesman* about the village, recalled:

> On the eastern bank of the reservoir, approximately a quarter of a mile from the reservoir embankment, was the original road leading to West End, which is now beneath the reservoir. This was Street Land, which linked Greenhow Hill Road by The Stone House Inn.

It is strangely comforting to know what lies down there, beneath the reservoir, but essentially, the vision of the loss and the erased past is just as powerful as the loss of Ravenser to many. History will, as always, emerge with a dozen differing perspectives and the truth will be obscured.

There is no such itinerary for Ravenser, Old Aldbrough or Dimlington. Science is basically saying, *leave it alone*, and business is saying, *defend those few hundred yards or else*. In the middle are those people with gardens the size of a notepad on the cliff edge, with their home behind, still bothering to mow the lawn, like the young man I saw in Hornsea. I like to think that sight could be a metaphor for what the human attitude has been through recorded history: nothing stops nature, so do what you can while you can.

That's a very Yorkshire attitude to life. It's built upon having the serenity to accept the things we cannot change, though it comes grudgingly, when all other choices fade away.

Acknowledgements

There have been several people around today who have helped with this project, but first credit has to go to someone from the past: the remarkable geologist and scholar, Thomas Sheppard, whose groundbreaking work on the lost towns made my work so much easier. His book (see the bibliography) is a marvellous mixture of geology, social history and documentary, and his illustrations have provided me with some of the rarest insights possible – material not even available on contemporary postcards. He was indeed an extraordinary character. M.R.D. Seaward points out that Sheppard held eighteen positions such as secretary, chairman or president on various society committees. He missed out conventional schooling and was an autodidact who acquired formidable levels of learning and scholarship. He died in 1945.

The other founding father of all knowledge of East Yorkshire is George Poulson (1783–1858), whose magnificent history of Holderness (see the bibliography) is indispensable for anyone looking into this subject. He used original records and unpublished manuscripts, including those of William Dade. Poulson also edited a social history of Barton on Humber.

Thanks also go to staff at the Brynmor Jones Library, University of Hull, and to staff at the History Centre, Hull. As in my social history research, thanks have to go to Bryan Longbone, the best consultant on railway history I know.

Glossary

As there have been so many terms used in the text, drawn from such diverse disciplines as geology, folklore, social history and economic history, it is helpful to the reader to have a simplified glossary. I have listed here only those words that, though briefly defined in the text, need more explanation. To have supplied this *in situ* would have marred the reading fluency, I feel.

Alum: A white mineral salt, mined on the Yorkshire coast, not only at Port Mulgrave but also north towards Teesside.

Boulder Clay: Clay with large stones, which was part of the terminal moraine of a glacier. After the movement of an ice sheet, the final extent of its reach, where it stopped, is the moraine.

Bronze Age: The period roughly from c.2500 BC to 500 BC. This followed the Neolithic period. Some early mining took place in this period, and there was a gradual opening up of copper mines in various regions.

Carr: This refers to a terrain that is at a stage between being forest and swamp. Star Carr in North Yorkshire is an important archaeological site.

Carucate: This is an alternative name for a hide: the amount of land that could theoretically be ploughed in a year with the use of just one plough.

Cleveland Basin: This is an area stretching from Malton in the south to Redcar in the north, mainly of Jurassic rock. This is on the edge of the great North Sea Basin, which extends across the sea, beyond the areas known as the Peak Trough and the Cayton Bay Fault System – out to sea beyond the northern section of the Yorkshire coast.

Close (sometimes 'cloise'): In Old French, this meant an enclosure or a field. In such things as rental records, this usually refers to a small area.

Coble: The distinctive fishing boat of the east coast, based on a Viking design. Before the 1950s, the cobles were taken into the sea pulled by horses. Michael Fearon writes: 'To launch a coble from the beach, or to bring it out of the water using three horses, was a skilful operation, especially when there were breakers of any size.' In an essay on the word 'coble', Eric Houlder gives a helpful definition of 'clinker built': 'Clinker construction involves the use of overlapping strakes (longitudinal planks) to make a shell into which the frames (ribs) are inserted. The strakes are fastened together with lines of clench-nails.'

Corrie: This is a feature caused by glaciation. The movement of a glacier can scoop up rock and form a hollow, and that usually fills with water and becomes a notable part of a landscape created by the events of an ice age.

Cwm: This is the Welsh word for 'valley', in general. But in geology, a cwm is a high or hanging valley, created by the movement of a glacier.

Danelaw: The area demarcated for the Viking settlers across eastern counties by the eleventh century. That area was influenced by Scandinavian law and tradition.

Doggerland: The great undersea area of former *carr* land, which formed a continuous land mass, bridging what is now the North Sea, about 10,000 years ago.

Domesday Book: William I's great land survey undertaken in his newly conquered domain of England, compiled by 1086. This provides mainly a record of land owners, and is also a register of title, so that William would know not simply what was owned but also something of the pedigree of the lords. The majority had been given land by him in 1066, but a lot could happen in twenty years!

Fault: A slip in a rock causing the creation of a lower level of rock. The Cayton Bay Fault System in the North Sea is a very large-scale example. It is specifically a dislocation of strata of rock or veins of minerals.

Geomorphology: The study of the creation and shaping of land forms. Clearly this is an important science when it comes to understanding, for instance, how erosion works or how sand moves and can engulf some areas.

Great Sand Drift, 1694: A massive movement of sand that engulfed a large extent of the Scottish coast in that year.

Grit/calcareous grit: A very small-sized rock fragment of coarse-grained sandstone. *Calcareous* refers to limy or *calcitic* rocks, calcite being the crystalline form of the calcium carbonate that is the basis of the formation of such things as fossils.

Hundred Roll: The hundred courts were established in the tenth century; they were run by the bailiffs in Saxon times, meeting every month. Their verdicts were recorded on the rolls.

Marram grass: A sea reed, which binds tightly to sand.

Mere: A sheet of standing water, a lake or a large pond (note – the modern German for 'sea' is das Meer). With so much settlement of Scandinavian people in the coastal lands, it comes as no surprise to see Germanic origins in much of Yorkshire dialect. The early Germanic language was the basis of all Scandinavian languages, except Finnish.

Mesolithic: The period roughly 10,500–5500 BC. As Tim Taylor explains in the handbook to the *Time Team* investigations, about the dwellers of the land at this time, 'Environmental studies have helped us piece together something of what happened on a geological and biological scale.' He adds, 'The archaeological and environmental evidence of this transition from Palaeolithic to Mesolithic is hard to identify. Most of the vast plains of the south east that would have been home to these nomadic people now rest under the North Sea.'

Northsealand: A name given by some archaeologists to Doggerland. It is useful, as it differentiates this undersea land from the fishing area of the Dogger Bank.

Neolithic: This refers to the later part of the Stone Age. The Star Carr investigations were within this period, around 8,000 BC.

Palaeolithic: This refers to the period c.650,00–10,500 BC.

Sandstone: A sedimentary rock that is largely made of sand-sized grains of quartz, a mineral.

Soccage: A freeholding of land without any imposition of the burden of having to do military service for the lord.

Soke: This was a word used in the Danelaw shires to denote an administrative area. It could extend across different manors.

Star Carr: This was basically a Mesolithic camp site. In spring and summer, the nomadic peoples of this period, before and during the ice retreat and the creation of the moraine, would have lived by hunting the deer and elk and other animals around the mere. When there were temporary homes, they appear to have been made of animal pelts over reed frames.

Till: Material left by glacial ice movement, of a mixed nature. This is vividly visible on the crumbling cliffs of so many coastal areas, where, if you stand close to the strata of rock and look closely at the composition of the material there, the mix of shells, fragments and fossils in the mud or clay will be plain to see.

Vill: This was a settlement of varying size, being anything from a parish to a manor.

Wapentake: A division of Yorkshire (and also some counties of East Anglia) similar to a *hundred*. The origin is from the Anglo–Saxon word meaning 'touch of a weapon' and this is explained in *Brewer's Dictionary of Phrase and Fable*: 'It being the custom of each vassal, when he attended the assemblies of the district to touch the spear of his overlord in token of homage.'

Sources and Bibliography

Note: Dates of first publication are given in the first brackets after the title.

Books/Works cited in the text

Anonymous, *Filey and District*, Ward Lock Guides, 1930.

Anonymous, *Trial and Innocence*, Ferens Art Gallery, 1984.

Arnold, Matthew, 'Dover Beach' in *The Penguin Book of English Verse*, Penguin, 2004, p.762.

Blass, Tom, *The Naked Shore*, Bloomsbury, 2015.

Burton, Thomas, *Chronicle of the Abbey of Meaux*, published in Latin in 1866–68, and then in English, Longmans Green, 1906.

Cavendish, Richard, *Explore Britain's Coastline*, Daily Telegraph Books, 1993.

Christian, Charles, *Yorkshire's Weird Wolds*, Kindle, 2015.

Crane, Nick, *Coast: Our Island Story*, BBC Books, 2012.

Crowther, Jan (Ed.), *Descriptions of East Yorkshire: De La Pryme to Head*, East Yorkshire Local History Society, 1992.

Crowther, Jan, *The People Along the Sand*, Phillimore, 2006.

Defoe, Daniel, *A Tour Through the Whole Island of Great Britain* (1724), Yale, 1991.

Fortey, Richard, *The Hidden Landscape*, Jonathan Cape, 1993.

Freethy, Ron, *Yorkshire: The Secret War 1939–1945*, Countryside Books.

Harlech, Lord, *Northern England: Illustrated Regional Guide to Ancient Monuments No.1*, HMSO, 1952.

Herbert, Barry, *Lifeboats of the Humber*, Hutton Press, 1991.

Hirst, Joseph H., *The Blockhouses of Kingston-upon-Hull*, A. Brown, 1913.

Holtby, Winifred, *South Riding* (1936), Random House, 2011.

Horan, Chris, *Humber Sail and History*, Chris Horan Editorial Services, 2010.

Irving, Henry, *The Tidal Havens of the Wash and the Humber*, Imray Laurie Norrie & Wilson, 1976.

Mayhall, John, *The Annals of Yorkshire*, Joseph Johnson, 1861.

Miles, David, *The Tale of the Axe*, Thames & Hudson, 2016.

Parkinson, Reverend Thomas, *Yorkshire Legends and Traditions as told by her Ancient Chroniclers* (1889), Hardpress, 2013.

Pennant, Thomas, see www.visionofbritain for his text of 'Scarborough to Berwick'.

Pontefract, Ella & Hartley, Marie, *Yorkshire Tour* (1939), Smith Settle, 2003.

Poulson, George, *The History and Antiquities of the Seignory of Holderness*, Robert Brown, 1840.

Pye, Michael, *The Edge of the World*, Penguin, 2014.

Rawson, P.F & Wright, J.K., *The Yorkshire Coast*, The Geologists' Association, 2000.

Richardson, John, *The Local Historian's Encyclopaedia*, Historical Publications, 1974.

Rotherham, Ian D., *Yorkshire's Forgotten Fenlands*, Pen & Sword, 2010.

Sheppard, Thomas, *Lost Towns of the Yorkshire Coast*, A. Brown & Sons, 1912.

Sheridan, Richard Brinsley, A Trip to Scarborough (1776), in *The School for Scandal and other plays*, OUP, 1998.

Smith, Graham, *Smuggling in Yorkshire*, Countryside Books, 1994.

Taylor, R.V., *Yorkshire Anecdotes*, Whittaker & Co., 1883.

Todd, Malcolm, *Roman Britain*, Fontana, 1985.

Troughton, Marion, *Pens, Profiles and Places*, Smith Settle, 1989.

Walford, Edward (Ed.), *Walford's Antiquarian*, George Redway, 1886.

Wayne, J.S., *The Diary of a Schoolboy*, transcribed by K. Clegg, K. Clegg, 1998.

Official Reports
HMSO Royal Commission on Coast Erosion and Afforestation, Wyman & Sons, 1911.

Reference Works
A History of the County of York North Riding Vol. 2, London, 1923.

Hanson, Lee (Ed.), *Edge of Heaven: The Yorkshire Coast*, Great Northern, 2011.

Kellett, Arnold, *The Yorkshire Dictionary*, Smith Settle, 1994.

Lagomarsino, James, *A Concise Guide to Rocks and Minerals*, Parragon, 2008.

Long, David, *Lost Britain*, Michael O'Mara, 2015.

Magnusson, Magnus & Palsson, Hermann, *King Harald's Saga*, Penguin, 1976.

Mathison, Phil, *The Spurn Gravel Trade*, Dead Good Publications.

Oliver, Neil, *A History of Ancient Britain*, Phoenix, 2012.

Oxford Dictionary of National Biography online.

Van der Noort, Robert & Davies, Paul, *Wetland Heritage*, Humber Wetland Project, 1993.

Westwood, Jennifer & Simpson, Jacqueline, *The Lore of the Land*, Penguin, 2005.

Articles in Periodicals/Contributions to Books
Anonymous, 'Jersey Knitters at Flamborough', *Hull Daily Mail*, 20 April 1928, p.6.

Anonymous, 'Monastic Chronicles of Meaux', *The Spectator*, 17 June 1871, p.19.

Anonymous, 'Lives may be at Risk if Sea Defences not Fixed', *Yorkshire Post*, 17 June 2016.

Burland, John, 'The Lost Village of West End', *The Dalesman*, September 2016, pp.46–9.

Francis, Tony, 'Terra non firma', *The Dalesman*, January 2015, pp.34–6.

Gallon, Andrew, 'A Perfect Peninsula', *The Dalesman*, March 2016, pp.24–8.

Houlder, Eric, 'Cobbles, Cobles and Setts', *The Dalesman*, September 2016, pp.68–9.

Howarth, M.K., 'The Jet Rock Series and the Alum Shale Series of the Yorkshire Coast', *Proceedings of the Yorkshire Geological Society*, Vol.33, Part 4, No.18, December 1962.

Haworth, Peter, 'The Smuggler's Revenge', in Whitworth, Alan (Ed.), *Aspects of the Yorkshire Coast 2*, Pen & Sword, 2000, pp.85–108.

Isaacson, Andy, 'Into Thin Ice', *National Geographic*, January 2016, Vol.229 No.1, pp.98–117.

Kirke, Roy, 'Witches, Wrecks and Windmills: Law and Order in Skipsea Parish up to the Twentieth Century', *East Yorkshire Historian*, No.5, 2004, pp.26–63.

Mellor, G.J., 'The Lost Seaside Piers of Yorkshire', *The Dalesman*, August 1964, pp.377–80.

Mitchell, W.R., 'Sea Parrots at Bempton', *The Dalesman Yorkshire Annual*, Dalesman Books, 1983, pp.25–9.

Joy, David, 'The Lost Port' in Hanson, Lee (Ed.), *The Edge of Heaven* (see above), pp.81–8.

Peach, Howard, 'The Man who Made Hornsea', *The Yorkshire Journal*, Summer 1999, pp.38–41.

Pearson, F.R., *Charlotte Bronte on the East Coast*, East Yorkshire Local History Society, 1957.

Taylor, R.V., 'Yorkshire Worthies', in *Old Yorkshire*, Longmans Green, 1881, pp.283–91.

Wheatley, David, 'Bubbling Under', in *The Dublin Review 63*, Summer 2006, p.6.

Wainwright, Martin, 'Yorkshire is Disappearing up to Three Times as Fast as Last year', *The Guardian*, 24 September, 2012.

Walker, John, 'Observations to Prove Filey Bay in Yorkshire, the *Portus felix* and Flamborough Head, the *ocellum Promontorium* of the Romans', *Archaeologia or Miscellaneous Tracts Relating to Antiquity*, Society of Antiquaries, 1834.

Walker, Peter, 'Tiny Mulgrave is not just any Port in a Storm', *Gazette and Herald*, 6 February, 2013.

Woodward, Anthony, 'The Riddle of the Sands', *Country Life*, August 2016, pp.34–41.

Archive materials/ Theses

Coast Protection Act, 1949, HMSO, 1972 version, with amendments.

Friend, Stephen, *A Sense of Belonging: Religion and Identity in Yorkshire and Humber Fishing Communities*, University of Hull, 2010.

Ms. Letters of the Baxter family: in the author's own archive.

The Coastal Handbook, The Environment Agency, June 2010.

Internet Sources

Anonymous, 'Coast Erosion', *Sheffield Daily Telegraph*, 11 November 1904, p.8. www.archaeology.co.uk.

'Beresford's Lost Villages', see www.dmv.hull.ac.uk.

Brigham, T. *Et alia*, 'Rapid Coastal Zone Assessment in Yorkshire and Lincolnshire', Humber Field Archaeology Report No.235, February 2008.

www.british-history.ac.uk. This has been a useful source for finding village descriptions from early travellers.

Calendar of Papal Registers 1373–1375, at British History Online (see above).

Clark, Chris & Robinson, Chris, 'Spittals Rock Survey 1997', The Filey Brigg Research group, see www.discoverfiley.org.

www.eastriding.gov.uk/coastalexplorer.

https:historicengland.org.uk/research. This site has the details of the geophysical survey undertaken by the National Mapping Programme.

'Land Reclamation, Sunk Island, Humber', *Hansard*, 10 March 1924, https://hansard.parliament.uk/.

www.hullgeolsoc.co.uk.

McKenzie, Steven, 'Buried Past: The Communities Lost to Sand'. See www.bbc.co.uk/news/uk-scotland-islands.

Mowthorpe, Ces, 'Dulcey Dock, Speeton Cliffs', see www.hunmanby.com/dulcey.html.

Norwood, Ernest Medforth, 'My Early Life in Kilnsea', at www.skeals.co.uk/Reminiscences/Ernie_Norwood.html.

www.nymcam.co.uk.

www.penelope.uchicago.edu. This is excellent for details of Ptolemy's mapping of Britain.

Rushton, John, 'Was there a Roman Port in Scarborough?', Scarborough Maritime Heritage Centre, www.scarboroughmaritimeheritage.org.

Seaward, M.R.D., 'The Amazing Mr Sheppard', Humberside Geologist Online, see www.hullgeolsoc.online.

See www.hullgeolsoc.co.uk. This is a lecture given to the Hull Geological Society in November 2008.

www.swell.org.uk.

www.sussex.ac.uk/geography/.

www.wilgilsland.co.uk. This gives a very full account of Kilnsea's essential history and also explains much of the social life – and some significant biographies.

Wright, Daniel L. & Herber, David, 'The Descendants of John Wright – Some Were Gunpowder Plotters', see www.gunpowderplot.org.

www.wonderfulwhitby.co.uk, 'Robin Hood's Bay'.

British Library Newspapers:
'Jersey Knitters at Flamborough', *Hull Daily Mail*, 20 April 1928, Issue 13,271.
'One Cottage Kitchen Goes Over the Top', *Nottingham Evening Post*, 4 January 1938, p.7, Issue 17,938.

Index